DRACULA
THE VAMPIRE LEGEND ON FILM

DRACULA
THE VAMPIRE LEGEND ON FILM

FANTASMA BOOKS

KEY WEST, FLORIDA

Published by Fantasma Books, 419 Amelia Street, Key West Florida 33040
United States of America

Library of Congress Catalog Card Number 92- 97128
ISBN 0-9634982-0-7

First American Edition

Cover Designed By Scott Jones

TABLE OF CONTENTS

INTRODUCTION

What is a vampire? The answer to this question varies on which movie you have just seen. In general terms and according to folklore and the definition provided in Webster's dictionary, a vampire is a corpse that simply becomes reanimated and sucks the blood of sleeping persons at night. An unscrupulous person who preys ruthlessly on others. Ruthless is the word, for the vampire is driven by only one desire: Human blood! They must have it to survive. The vampire is not driven by friendship or love, although there have been rare instances during cinema history when a vampire has put love before blood as in THE GREAT LOVE OF COUNT DRACULA (1972), BLACULA (1971) and TO DIE FOR (1988). However, the vampire normally does not care who you are (brother, sister, mother, father, son or daughter) as long as your blood is warm. Regardless of its sexual nature, involvement with a vampire always spells death. The vampire strikes ruthlessly from the dark like a lightening bolt and usually without warning. Afterwards, all that remains of the victim is a bloody mess.

Now it is very important that you understand that there are vampires and then there are "The Vampires!" Count Dracula has always been and will always be the Vampire King. He is the Prince of Darkness and the Ruler of The Undead. He walks hand and hand with Satan himself. He is ruthless, cunning and very, very evil; an intelligent beast whose handsome features and polished gentlemen-like qualities will fool you every time. With master vampires, however, there are exceptions, as in both versions of NOSFERATU (1922 & 1979). In these films, Dracula was portrayed as a hideous rat-like monster with fowl breath, long claws, pointy ears and protruding fangs. When we think of Count Dracula on film, Bela Lugosi and Christopher Lee usually come to mind. And why not. Their films have helped shaped the image of this great fiend in our minds. Both Lugosi and Lee's Dracula characterizations are regarded as the screen's greatest and Universal's DRACULA (1931) and Hammer's HORROR OF DRACULA (1958) are regarded as milestones in the genre. Dracula was born in 1896, when Bram Stoker published his infamous book Dracula. Stoker based his Transylvanian character on the legendary and historical warrior Vlad Tepes. The author combined history with the vampire folklore to create the greatest vampire of them all. Since the advent of film, Dracula has become the screen's most popular vampire, beginning in 1922 with NOSFERATU, through the 1930's and 1940's with Bela Lugosi and on through 1960's with Christopher Lee up through 1992 with BRAM STOKER'S DRACULA from Francis Ford Coppola. In a word, Count Dracula is supreme.

Another legendary literary and movie vampire is the sultry female Carmilla, also known as Mircalla and Countess Karnstein. Whatever name she presents herself as, she is still very deadly, proving that the female species is as lethal as the male species. The lesbian vampire usually seduces her victim, then slowly drains their life away providing her with erotic and sensual pleasures as well a her nourishment. Carmilla has been known to drain the blood of females through their private parts, as in Hammer's LUST FOR A VAMPIRE (1971). She has made numerous appearances in film, including VAMPYR (1932), BLOOD AND ROSES (1960) and THE VAMPIRE LOVERS (1970), and even a film with her name as a title, CARMILLA (1989). But the films that really stick out in the mind are those graphic Hammer films made during the early 1970's. The legend of Carmilla was created by writer Sheridan Le Fanu in his novel, also entitled Carmilla. She is indeed the screen's leading female vampire.

Then there is Countess Elizabeth Bathory, the legendary noblewoman who use to slaughter young virgins for their blood. But this creature did not drink the blood. Instead, she bathed in it, claiming that the blood of virgin girls kept her youthful appearance. Hollywood has since then given her the nickname of Countess Dracula, and her legend has been intermingled with other vampire films throughout history. Bathory made her claim in cinema as a leading female vamp in Hammer's COUNTESS DRACULA (1971) and carried on the tradition in such films as THE DEVIL'S WEDDING NIGHT (1973) and THE CRAVING (1980), to name just a few.

Of course, there are many other master vampires to be reckoned with, such as the infamous

Barnabas Collins of HOUSE OF DARK SHADOWS (1970); Count Yorga of COUNT YORGA-VAMPIRE (1970); Nostradamus and Lavud of the Mexican vampire films;   Baron Meinster of BRIDES OF DRACULA (1960); Blacula from BLACULA (1971); Jerry Dandridge of FRIGHT NIGHT (1985);   Kiefer Sutherland's vampire in THE LOST BOYS (1987);   and Grace Jones's sultry vampiress in VAMP (1988).   These are just a few of the many creatures of the night that have graced the screen with their savage and bloodthirsty presence, and they only represent a handful of the many others that have frightened us over the years.

There is also the matter of folklore to be considered when defining the vampire.   For the most part, the cinema has always depicted vampires as nocturnal creatures, beginning with NOSFERATU (1922) and continuing through films like FRIGHT NIGHT (1985), NEAR DARK (1987), THE LOST BOYS (1987) and of course, GRAVEYARD SHIFT (Parts One and Two!).   But screenwriters have a knack for changing the rules around.   In Hammer's KISS OF THE VAMPIRE (1963), the central vampire was allowed to walk in broad daylight hours during an overcast day and with an umbrella.   In fact, Frank Langella's vampire in DRACULA (1979) made an appearance on his horse just before sunset. Could this have been an oversight?   Then there are those horrible low budget Mexican films in which the filmmakers slip and allow the vampire to be seen in the light of day.   A definite oversight!

What about the part of the legend dictating that vampires cannot cast an image in a mirror.   Well, putting those Mexican films aside, didn't James Mason cast an image in SALEM'S LOT (1979)?   He was vampirized.   How about the vampire in FRIGHT NIGHT (1985)?

How about running water?   This addition to the myth became part of the legend in Hammer's DRACULA - PRINCE OF DARKNESS (1965).   In fact, running water actually killed Christopher Lee's Dracula in that film, as well as Christopher Neame's vampire in DRACULA A.D.-1972 (1971).

How about crucifixes?   According to the legend, crucifixes are suppose to repel these predators of the night like a can of Off chases away mosquitoes.   In SALEM'S LOT (1979), the crucifix didn't seem to bother the Barlow the vampire, nor did it repel Frank Langella's vampire in DRACULA (1979). Yet, I can remember on many occasions Bela Lugosi, Lon Chaney, Jr. and Christopher Lee's vampires fearing the almighty crucifix in DRACULA (1931), SON OF DRACULA (1943) and HORROR OF DRACULA (1958).

Here's a good contradiction to the legend.   Screenwriters really changed the rules around in Hammer's DRACULA HAS RISEN FROM THE GRAVE (1968).   In this flick, Christopher Lee's Dracula is impaled with a wooden stake through his heart while resting in his coffin during daylight hours. Under normal circumstances and according to the legend set forth by the traditional Universal movies, that would have been it for that vampire.   He would have been ashes and bones as in the case of John Carradine's Dracula in HOUSE OF FRANKENSTEIN (1944).   Dracula would have been history.   NOT!   Because the film's hero was an atheist he was unable to pray, therefore the vampire was able to remove the stake before dying.   Ever since then, certain vampire films have used the theory that you must have faith in God in order to repel or kill a vampire, as in TASTE THE BLOOD OF DRACULA (1969), SALEM'S LOT (1979) and FRIGHT NIGHT (1985), to name only a few.   You see, screenwriters have a knack for changing the folklore around a bit.

Now we come to the bloody part of this section: How vampires feed! In the old days it was simple. The vampire would traditionally bite their victim on the neck.   The effect was usually achieved by using shadows.   This was usually enough to send audiences into a panic.   The vampire's feeding habits progressively became a little more sloppy and messy when Christopher Lee made his debut as Count Dracula in HORROR OF DRACULA (1958).   For the first time, we were able to see a vampire physically feeding.   In one of cinema's most graphic moments, Lee's Dracula penetrated his victim's neck with his fangs and he began to drink their blood.   Of course, for the film's dramatic effect, some of the blood trickled down the victim's neck and smeared all over the vampire's lips. This new wave of blood lust continued on through many vampire films since then,   with Hammer's LUST FOR A VAMPIRE (1971) and VAMPIRE CIRCUS (1971) and Andy Warhol's BLOOD FOR DRACULA (1973) being the most graphic of the lot. Each decade demanded more blood, more splatter and more violence. This is evident by the films themselves. Of course, Hollywood has always demanded change in folklore, and soon we were finding vampires obtaining their nourishment in the most unusual ways. For example, in A RETURN TO SALEM'S LOT (1987), the vampires drank the blood of farm animals, while in NOT OF THIS EARTH (1988), TO DIE FOR PART II (1991) and NIGHTLIFE (1990) they obtained their food from blood transfusions and blood banks. In LIFE FORCE (1985), the alien vampire sucked the energy force out of humans, turning them to zombies, while in RABID (1976), the vampire used a penis-like extension from under her arm pit to drain her victims of their blood, turning them into rabid-like homicidal maniacs. Whatever the method used to obtain blood, the vampire will stop at nothing until it has received the nourishment needed to maintain its existence.

In writing this book, I have tried to cover every vampire film known to exist. Here you will find the best and the worst vampire films. You will find the traditional, the unusual and the obscure vampire movies. You will find vampire movies made in Hollywood and from different countries around the world. Each film is chronologically listed according to their release dates. If you wish to find a specific title and are not certain of the year the film was released, you can look up the film alphabetically in the film index located at the back of this book. And if you know of a vampire film that has not been covered in this book, please write me directly so that I may add it to the next edition of this volume. You may send your comments to the publisher's address in my attention. And remember, when reading this book, don't let the bed bats bite! Lock your windows and close your doors. ENJOY!!!!!!

Robert Marrero
Author

8

70 YEARS OF VAMPIRE MOVIES

FROM 1922 TO 1992

NOSFERATU, A SYMPHONY OF TERROR

Prana 1922

This silent masterpiece of horror is the first screen adaptation of Bram Stoker's famous novel, Dracula, published in 1897. The film is directed by one of Germany's greatest expressionistic filmmakers, F.W. Murnau. To avoid paying royalties to the copyright owners of Dracula the novel, Murnau changed the names of the characters and the film's setting. Count Dracula became Count Orlock; Jonathan Harker became Waldemar Hutter; Van Helsing became Professor Bulwer; and Renfield was changed to Knock. The story was changed from Transylvania to Germany, and Bremen was substituted for London. Despite the name changes in characters and the setting changes, the premise remained relatively the same as the novel. In fact the screenplay by Henrik Galeen is more faithful to the Stoker novel than both the later versions made by Universal and Hammer. The most drastic difference from the Stoker novel and this film is the vampire's physical appearance. Count Orlock, portrayed by actor Max Schreck, is portrayed as a bald, human rodent-type creature, who rises from his foul smelling grave. Unlike Stoker's mysterious and handsome noble character, Orlock wore no tuxedo or cloak, nor did he bid fair maidens welcome. Instead, he preyed upon innocent victims like a bubonic plague, satisfying his unquenchable thirst for human blood. Orlock was and still is the most hideous vampire ever to prowl the screen. With pointed ears, pale face, razor sharp teeth and claws, the Hellish demon leads his legions of rats from the subterranean levels of Germany and sails to Breman where a terrible plague strikes the town. The demon vampire is eventually destroyed when the film's heroine sacrifices her own life and soul to the vampire. She keeps Orlock occupied till sunrise, until he perishes from exposure to the sun's lethal rays. NOSFERATU was never given wide distribution. The film's faithfulness to the Stoker novel forced it out of circulation because of copyright infringements enforced by Florence Stoker. Murnau was compelled to withdraw the film in July 1925. Today, NOSFERATU is considered by film historians as one of the greatest horror films ever made, and the film is by far one of the greatest vampire tales to ever hit the screen and a timeless classic.

LONDON AFTER MIDNIGHT

MGM 1927

During the mid 1920's, American film companies became more involved with the growing genre of horror films. Actor Lon Chaney, Sr. was the leading horror film star at a time long before Bela Lugosi and Boris Karloff rose to fame. Chaney was most famous for his monstrous movie characterizations in THE HUNCHBACK OF NOTRE DAME (1923) and THE PHANTOM OF THE OPERA (1925). In 1927, the actor played a pseudo-vampire in the first American vampire film, LONDON AFTER MIDNIGHT. The film was based on the novel The Hypnotist by Tod Browning, who also wrote and directed the film. The film leads the viewer to believe that there really is a vampire (played by Chaney) running around an old castle, when really the vampire is revealed as being a police detective in disguise during the film's climax. The vampire trappings were staged throughout the film to frighten a murderer into disclosing his involvement with a killing. Chaney assumed both the roles of the detective and the vampire, and the audiences of 1927 were subject to the hoax. Despite the prank, Chaney's vampire is quite impressive, and the supernatural elements prior to the revelation of the hoax are quite effective. One can only wonder how Chaney's Count Dracula would have been depicted had he portrayed the character in the Universal classic of 1931. Chaney died in 1930.

DRACULA

Universal 1931

Lon Chaney, Sr. died in 1930, and so did his chance to portray Bram Stoker's legendary vampire, Count Dracula in this, the granddaddy of all vampire films. The role naturally went to Hungarian-born actor Bela Lugosi. To this day, no other actor is most associated with the name Count Dracula than Bela Lugosi. Lugosi is the epitome of the classic, handsome, suave and debonair vampire count. Lugosi's Dracula is cunning and clever and very resourceful with centuries of knowledge at his disposal. His vampire is mysterious and romantic, a polished gentlemen turned into a living monster. In the film, you never really see Lugosi sucking the blood from his victim. This was all left to the audiences' imaginations. Director Tod Browning is capable of creating the supernatural elements off screen, and the film heavily relies on the actors and the massive sets and stylish camera work of Karl Freund to establish its eerie Gothic atmosphere. DRACULA follows the story line of Bram Stoker's novel relatively close, beginning with Jonathan Harker's arrival at Castle Dracula in Transylvania. Count Dracula naturally devours the Englishman, as he has done with most of his countrymen, and sets sail to England, where he begins sinking his teeth into the necks of Englishmen and seducing young maidens with his mysterious charm. As the vampire carries out his evil doings, he is eventually revealed as the monster he really is by his arch nemesis Professor Van Helsing (played by Edward Van Sloan). The dialogue and confrontations between the two arch enemies is brilliant and satisfying. The entire film is breathtaking, and one of the greatest horror films ever made. DRACULA is a relic of an era long vanished and one of cinema's true masterpieces.

DRACULA

Universal 1931 (Spanish)

With the enormous success of DRACULA `(1931), Universal produced a Spanish version of the film directed by George Melford. The film stars Carlos Villarias as Count Dracula. Villarias has an uncanny resemblance to Bela Lugosi, and like his counterpart, he makes an effective Dracula. The same sets were salvaged from the original. This version is almost always overlooked by fans of horror films.

VAMPYR

Independent (German) 1932

Loosely based on the novella Carmilla by Sheridan LeFanu VAMPYR is regarded as one of the true masterpieces of the golden horror film. Atmospherically photographed by cinematographer Rudolph Mate for director Carl Dreyer, the film very subtly tells the story of a man's (played by Julian West, who also produced the film) journey to a small village that is plagued by an old female vampire (played by Henriette Gerard). Dreyer uses strong symbolisms to establish the mood, such as a nightmare sequence in which the hero imagines himself buried alive in a coffin with the vampire lady peering at him through the lid's transom. The scene is still most frightening, as the camera

replaces his position in the casket, giving us the feeling that we are also enclosed with the hero. Photographer Mate shot the entire film through a special gauze lens to create the dream-like effect and Dreyer only shot the film during dusk and dawn. The film was given a very limited release in America. American distributors felt that audiences would not appreciate the subtle qualities of the film after having enjoyed such traditional horror films as Universal's DRACULA and FRANKENSTEIN (Both 1931). In hindsight, the distributors were correct.

THE VAMPIRE BAT

Majestic 1933

Directed by Frank Strayer on a low budget, THE VAMPIRE BAT stars Lionel Atwill as scientist Otto Von Niemann. In the film, Atwill perpetrates a hoax that a vampire is killing the townspeople when in actuality, it is he who is draining the blood of the villagers to keep his experiments alive while his servant Emil (played by Robert Fraser) wears a flowing cloak at night as he seeks his victims. The villagers suspect a lunatic vampire bat keeper named Herman (played by Dwight Frye). The film did not fare well next to Universal's DRACULA and FRANKENSTEIN (1931), and when viewed today, appears very dated. But Frye is excellent once again as a lunatic and Atwill delivers his sinister lines with such great enjoyment that his overall performance glows.

MARK OF THE VAMPIRE

MGM 1935

With the success of DRACULA (1931) and FREAKS (1932) behind him, director Tod Browning set out to remake his previous pseudo-vampire classic LONDON AFTER MIDNIGHT (1927). MARK OF THE VAMPIRE is indeed a remake of the Lon Chaney classic, however it offers many of the characteristics of Universal's DRACULA, primarily because the film stars Bela Lugosi as Count Mora, the pseudo vampire. Universal's DRACULA had not yet been produced

when LONDON AFTER MIDNIGHT was released, therefore the original has a style and mood all of its own, whereas MARK OF THE VAMPIRE was made under the influence of DRACULA, to capitalize on its success. Like the original, MARK OF THE VAMPIRE uses its vampire and its vampire elements of the film to disclose a murderer. The entire scheme is the brainstorm of inspector Neumann (played by Lionel Atwill), and like the original, the scheme works, but the hoax, however, does not. By 1935, audiences were spoiled by the likes of real monsters in DRACULA, FRANKENSTEIN (1931), THE MUMMY (1932) and THE WEREWOLF OF LONDON (1935). These monsters were not a hoax, at least, not in film terms. MARK OF THE VAMPIRE was considered a let down, but before the vampires are revealed as actors, Browning does deliver some very eerie moments that actually surpass many of the trappings used in DRACULA, thus the film should not be judged so harshly. The film is a first rate Gothic thriller right up to the hoax and although he does not deliver any dialogue, Lugosi is brilliant in establishing the mood of the film.

DRACULA'S DAUGHTER

Universal 1936

Universal was very good at making sequels to its original horror films, and DRACULA'S DAUGHTER is actually a very competent sequel to DRACULA even though the film lacks the key personality of such superstars as Bela Lugosi and Boris Karloff. DRACULA'S DAUGHTER is smoothly directed by Lambert Hillyer from a script written by Garrett Fort and based on the novel Dracula's Guest by Bram Stoker. Although the film was produced on a lower than normal budget by Universal standards during the early to mid 1930's, DRACULA'S DAUGHTER appears to be an expensive film. Cast in the title role is the beautiful actress Gloria Holden. As Countess Marya Zaleska, the ill-fated daughter of Count Dracula, Holden is tempted by the film's real villain, her evil manservant Sandor (played by Irving Pichel). In the film, Sandor influences the Countess to perform acts of vampirism because he fears that she will not fullfil her promise of making him immortal. Universal has managed to produce a beautifully atmospheric vampire tale that offers continuity with the original film. Actor Edward Van Sloan reprises his role as Professor Van Helsing and co-star Otto Kruger makes a good vampire killer. The film clearly represents the end of an era of quality horror films produced by Universal Pictures during the early to mid 1930's. Universal would never make another Gothic horror film quite as technically good as evident by the studio's horror films that followed.

THE RETURN OF DR. X

Warner   1939

Humphrey Bogart starred in only one horror picture in his entire career, and THE RETURN OF DR. X was that film. Apparently, Bogart was forced into the picture as part of a multi-film contract with Warner. The actor hated the idea of sitting in a make-up chair for two hours prior to filming and an additional two hours following filming to remove the make-up. Incidentally, the make-up for Bogart's vampire was created by make-up artist Perc Westmore. Bogart's lack of enthusiasm shows in his bland performance as the vampiric Dr. Xavier. The film, directed by Vincent Sherman, is an entire waste of the actor's talents, as well as actors Wayne Morris, Dennis Morgan and Rosemary Lane. Furthermore, the misleading title suggests that the film is a sequel to the classic horror film DR. X (1932) with Lionel Atwill, also from Warner. This is not the case. Bogart delivers what is one of film history's worse performance as a vampire.

SON OF DRACULA

Universal   1943

During the late 1930's and the early 1940's, Universal Pictures launched a new series of monster movies and new horror film stars to alter its image. The studio began by grooming Lon Chaney, Jr. as Bela Lugosi and Boris Karloff's replacement in a series of horror films that included MAN MADE MONSTER (1940), THE WOLFMAN (1941), THE GHOST OF FRANKENSTEIN (1941) and THE MUMMY'S TOMB (1942). The actor was also given the opportunity to portray the new Dracula in SON OF DRACULA. The studio made an unwise decision in choosing Chaney over Bela Lugosi, for he was to awkward and brute an actor to take on the part of a suave and debonair Count Alucard (Dracula spelled backwards) in this sequel to DRACULA'S DAUGHTER (1936). The role should have went to Lugosi, or even to actor John Carradine, who would later don the cloak and name of Dracula for Universal. In any event, the awkward performance of Lon Chaney is overcome by the fast-paced and entertaining direction of Robert Siodmak, whose only concern is to provide action and thrills, as he does ever so well with this picture. The film relies more on the visual effects of John P. Fulton rather than the dialogue of Eric Taylor's weak script. To begin with, the script removes the setting from Transylvania to a southern plantation in America, where the vampire seduces his lovely and very willing hostess (played by Louise Albritton). As Count Alucard, Chaney is pursued by a Professor Van Helsing-type authority on vampires named Professor Lazlo (played by J. Edwards Bromberg). There are many flaws in SON OF DRACULA, but for those who enjoy good old fashion entertainment, the film delivers in which case Chaney's brutal characterization of Count Dracula is overshadowed.

RETURN OF THE VAMPIRE

Columbia   1943

While Universal had Lon Chaney as Count Dracula, Columbia Pictures launched a series of " B " horror films beginning with Boris Karloff's mad scientist films and continuing with Bela Lugosi's RETURN OF THE VAMPIRE. In this film, Lugosi portrays Armand Tessla, a vampire virtually similar to his Dracula characterization of 1931. Tessla is a student of the occult turned into a vampire. With the aide of his werewolf servant Andreas (played by Matt Willis), the vampire sets out after those who destroyed him many years ago. However, when both monsters fall in love with actress Nina Foch, they battle each other to their deaths. The film is directed by Lew Landers in a style reminiscent of Universal's FRANKENSTEIN MEETS THE WOLFMAN (1943) in which both monsters battle each other during the mighty climax. The teaming of movie monsters seemed to be the profitable thing to do during the 1940's and RETURN OF THE VAMPIRE was produced to capitalize on this market. Despite the film's low production values, RETURN OF THE VAMPIRE does offer some very effective moments as a horror film, primarily the scene in which Lugosi's vampire claws his way out of his grave. RETURN OF THE VAMPIRE is probably the best of the " B " vampire films from the 1940's and 1950's.

DEAD MEN WALK

PRC   1943

Actor Dwight Frye was excellent as demented dwarfs and grave diggers in films such as DRACULA (1931), FRANKENSTEIN (1931) and THE VAMPIRE BAT (1933). In DEAD MEN WALK, Frye gives another Renfield-type performance, this time as Zolar, the hunchback servant of George Zucco's vampire. The film was PRC's first and final vampire film, and as typical of these films, there is no atmosphere, no character development, cheap sets and very little budget. The film was directed without any style by Sam Newfeld.

HOUSE OF FRANKENSTEIN

Universal   1944

Writers Curt Siodmak and Edward T. Lowe had exhausted every conceivable original idea for a new horror film before coming up with the idea of combining the studio's most famous monsters in one film. In the film, the Frankenstein Monster (Glenn Strange), the Wolfman (Lon Chaney), the Mad Scientist (Boris Karloff), the hunchback assistant (J. Carrol Naish) and Count Dracula (John Carradine) have a field day with their victims. Count Dracula is revived from his skeletal remains when Karloff removes a stake that once sent the vampire king into limbo. Now fully revived, Dracula is promised victims by Karloff in return for doing the mad scientist's evil bidding. Dracula disguises himself as Baron Latos and eventually begins working for himself. The vampire seduces and abducts actress Ann Gwyne with intentions of making her his mistress and part of the undead world. In a fast-paced cross country chase with the police staged during the early part of the film, the vampire becomes a victim to the sun's rays and decomposes before he can reach the safety of his coffin. The film is directed in a hurried fashion by Robert H. Oliver and uses the Dracula legend to link the other monsters into the film. The real star was the Frankenstein Monster, but Carradine's Dracula made a great impression. One wonders how well a film HOUSE OF FRANKENSTEIN could have been with Boris Karloff as the Mad Scientist, Lon Chaney as the Wolfman and Bela Lugosi as Count Dracula. I suppose we shall never know.

HOUSE OF DRACULA

Universal 1945

A direct sequel to HOUSE OF FRANKENSTEIN in which actor John Carradine returns to the role of Count Dracula. In the film, Dracula announces himself again as Baron Latos and uses Mad Scientist Onslow Stevens to find a cure to his vampiric condition, however the vampire's plans go haywire when Stevens gives most of his attention to curing Lon Chaney's werewolf condition and reviving the Frankenstein Monster (played once again by Glenn Strange). To make matters worse, Stevens inadvertently turns himself into a Jekyll-Hyde monster after a failed blood transfusion with Dracula. Once again, Count Dracula perishes at the mercy of the sun's lethal rays. Although Carradine's

Dracula was given more footage in HOUSE OF DRACULA, the film was Universal's shortest running horror film and a final farewell to their monster creations. The film ended a generation of monster movies that once dominated the screen.

THE VAMPIRE'S GHOST

Republic 1945

Republic Pictures typically produced " B" horror and western films during the 1940's, and THE VAMPIRE'S GHOST is a typical example of how the studio would exploit a genre. In the film, actor John Abbott is a centuries old vampire cursed since Elizabethan times in the west coast of Africa. Abbott's vampire did not sleep in a coffin as did his traditional ancestors. Instead, he carried a minature casket with some native soil. By day, the vampire sports around with dark sunglasses, doomed by an ancient curse to roam the Earth throughout eternity. The film just does not have the budget nor the time (59 minutes) to develop any type of atmosphere and uses cheap thrills to satisfy its audience. The screen treatment by Leigh Brackett is weak and Lesley Selander's direction is aimed towards action and suspense rather than the film's characters. Much better was Columbia's " B" films RETURN OF THE VAMPIRE (1943) and CRY OF THE WEREWOLF .

ABBOTT AND COSTELLO MEET FRANKENSTEIN

Universal Intl. 1948

The horror film cycle had ended for Universal with HOUSE OF DRACULA, but the old monsters were called upon one last time to chill audiences alongside the studio's then top box office draw Bud Abbott and Lou Costello. The film cleverly combines the comedy antics of Abbott and Costello with that of the horrors created by the Frankenstein Monster (Glenn Strange), The Wolfman (Lon Chaney) and Count Dracula (Bela Lugosi). Yes, Bela Lugosi was finally given a break by the big studio, and his performance as Count Dracula some seventeen years after

DRACULA (1931) is as mysterious and fascinating as was his original characterization. Lugosi, donning his famous black cape and tuxedo, has fiendish plans of reviving the Frankenstein Monster at the expense of Abbott's brain. Although the plot is feeble in how the monsters are used, the film is quite entertaining, though dated, and Bela gives a distinguished farewell performance as the vampire King. The success of ABBOTT AND COSTELLO MEET FRANKENSTEIN actually saved the declining careers of Bud Abbott and Lou Costello but was unfortunately not enough to save the old horror monsters from a new horizon of horror films.

OLD MOTHER RILEY MEETS THE VAMPIRE

Renown Pictures 1952

Director John Gilling's tale about a mad scientist (played by Bela Lugosi) who tries to control the world by creating an army of lethal robots has really nothing to do with the vampire legend. In fact, the word vampire in the title is explained away in the script as Lugosi's fantasies. In the film he sleeps in a coffin and expresses his desire for human blood. Lugosi does wear his black tuxedo and Dracula cape, but this is all a ploy to develop his character's deranged image. Poor Lugosi was only paid $5,000 for his role in this film, which was released in Great Britain by Renown first and then in America in 1963 under the misleading title MY SON, THE VAMPIRE.

DRAKULA IN ISTANBUL

And Films 1953

Turkish version of the Bram Stoker novel and the novel Kasigli Voyvoda by Ali Riga Seifi directed by Mehmet Muhtar. This impressive version of the legend stars Atif Kaptan, bald and grey and bearing unusual fangs, as Drakula, bald and grey and bearing unusual fangs. The plot generally follows that of the Stoker book. An accountant named Amzi journeys to Castle Drakula in the Carpathian Mountains to become the nobleman's personal secretary.

Amzi is greeted by the Count's hunchback assistant and at sunset, he meets Drakula himself. Amzi discovers that Drakula is a vampire when he locates the fiend slumbering in a coffin. Amzi manages to flee the castle, but Drakula soon follows him to Istanbul and begins to terrorize his family, enticing his fiance and transforming her into a vampire too. Accompanied by a Turkish version of Van Helsing, Amzi locates Drakula's secret resting place and the heroic duo drives a wooden stake through his heart and then beheads the beast.

EL VAMPIRO

Cinematografica   1956

This Mexican-made vampire film is the one that started it all for Mexico! Directed by Fernando Mendez, EL VAMPIRO stars actor German Robles as Count Lavud, a carbon copy of Bela Lugosi's Dracula image. The Count is also equipped with a set of fangs and dressed in a tuxedo and cape with a royal medallion hung over his chest. A young girl named Marta (Ariadna Welter) visits a farm owned by her two elderly aunts. She soon discovers that one of them is under the spell of a mysterious Count Lavud who, at the beginning of the film goes under the name of Mr. Duval (another backwards spelling a copy of Alucard). The other aunt mysteriously dies, drained of all her blood, and soon Marta is at risk. Later, Marta discovers that her un-living aunt casts no reflection. Her aunt slips her a drug that gives her the semblance of death. Marta is nearly buried alive when a kind doctor saves her, resulting in another attack by the vampire. The doctor and the vampire battle one another leading to another stake in the heart. Director Mendez's Gothic atmosphere is very satisfying and almost worthy of many of the American films of the same nature.

THE VAMPIRO'S COFFIN

Cinematografica   1957

EL VAMPIRO was so successful in Mexico that producers were highly interested in following-up the film with this sequel, also directed by Fernando Mendez.   In this film, a mad scientist and his assistant steal the impaled corpse of Count Lavud and accidentally remove the stake to steal the vampire's medallion. This revives the creature who is determined to recapture his Marta (again played by Ariadna Welter) from the first film. During the film's climax, Count Lavud manages to transform into a bat to escape the doctor's silver blade, but the good doctor does manage to pin the bat against the wall with the thrust of a javelin. The vampire regains his human form, pinned to the wall, where he dies slowly.   THE VAMPIRO'S COFFIN offers some impressive shadow photography, and the confrontation between the film's savant doctor and the vampire is as impressive as their previous encounters, considering the low production values. The sequel also ended the series of Count Lavud films from Mexico, but actor German Robles did go on to portray other cinematic vampires for Mexico.

BLOOD OF DRACULA

AIP   1957

During the mid to late 1950's, filmmaker Herbert L. Strock started a sensation by directing low budget horror films that used teenagers as their focal characters and monsters. Naturally, these films were marketed to the nation's youth as well as hard-core horror movie fans and included such memorable titles as I WAS A TEENAGE WEREWOLF (1957), I WAS A TEENAGE FRANKENSTEIN (1957), THE BLOB (1959) and many others. BLOOD OF DRACULA was Strock's teenage version of the vampire legend. The film is misleading in that neither Dracula nor his blood is ever featured anywhere throughout this film. In fact, the teenage vampire in the film was not even from Transylvania. Sandra Harrison plays a neurotic Nancy Perkins, who is enrolled into an all girls school. There she is coerced into wearing a centuries-old medallion that once belonged to a very powerful vampire (Dracula?) by a suspicious old chemistry teacher. The amulet causes the teenager to transform into a bloodthirsty human vampire with long bushy eyebrows and two elongated fangs, as created by make-up artist Philip Scheer. The film should have been called DRACULA'S MEDALLION, but somehow BLOOD OF DRACULA sounds much more enticing.

THE VAMPIRE

United Artists   1957

In THE VAMPIRE from producers Jules Levy and Arthur Gardner, actor John Beal undergoes a transformation into a bloodthirsty vampire when a scientist subjects him to a new kind of pill. Whenever the moon rises, Beal becomes a puffy-faced monster who disposes of his victims in a furnace. The low budget thriller was directed by Paul Landres, who also directed RETURN OF DRACULA (1958).

RETURN OF DRACULA (1958)

United Artists   1958

More traditional than THE VAMPIRE (1957) is Levy, Gardner and Landres' RETURN OF DRACULA. The film starred handesome Czechoslovakian actor Francis Lederer as a curly-haired Count Dracula. The vampire drains the blood of a fellow country-man named Bellac Gordal, who prepares to leave to America to meet his never before seen relatives. Dracula assumes Bellac's identity and travels to a small American village where he terrorizes the poor dead man's relatives. Francis Lederer is refreshing as Dracula for those who have not yet seen this film, and the plot is quite original and undated by today's standards. The theme of transplanting Dracula from centuries-old Transylvania to the American midwest works much better here than in Universal's SON OF DRACULA (1943), where the Count (Alucard)   is transposed to the American south.   The vampire's destruction in which Dracula falls into a deep pit and onto a wooden shaft is quite effective, but somehow this very good film seems anemic next to Hammer's classic and colorful adaptation of Bram Stoker's novel Dracula released the same year in America as HORROR OF DRACULA.

HORROR OF DRACULA

Hammer   1958

By the late 1950's, the traditional movie monsters that once haunted the Universal lot during the previous decades, were quickly fading into just memories. In 1957, a British based film company began filming Gothic horror movies in color, bringing life and popularity back to the vintage monsters of the golden age of cinema. What Universal had once concealed in atmospheric shadows or in characters reacting to offscreen supernatural occurrences, Hammer exposed in full light and in vivid and colorful close-ups. Hammer used generous helpings of red color in their films to create mood. In 1957, the studio made CURSE OF FRANKENSTEIN, a color remake of the 1931 Universal classic. The film raked in big bucks at the box office, and executive producer James Carreras commissioned screenwriter Jimmy Sangster to write a new script based on Bram Stoker's Dracula. Sangster's main objective was to focus on the physical characteristics of Dracula, as portrayed convincingly in this film by British actor Christopher Lee. Lee's Dracula is incredibly handsome but totally evil and corrupt, with only one thing on his mind, human blood! This Dracula was dynamic instead of subttle, colorful, instead of grey, and very much "alive!" Lee's Dracula, dressed in black formal wear with a red-lined black cloak, is the most fiendish, cunning and powerful vampire ever. HORROR OF DRACULA is stylishly directed by Terence Fisher and follows the Stoker novel faithfully, to a degree. In the film, Jonathan Harker (John Van Eyssen) is sent to Castle Dracula in Transylvania by Professor Van Helsing (Peter Cushing). Harker poses as a British librarian who arrives to the castle to apply for the opening of Dracula's librarian position (this was probably Dracula's way of luring fresh victims to his castle from faraway places). Harker meets a horrible death when he tries to destroy the vampiric Count, and soon Professor Van Helsing arrives to discover that his friend has suffered a horrible fate. Dracula travels to London and hides in the catacombs of a large estate where he makes the move on Harker's fiance. The climax of HORROR OF DRACULA is one of the greatest and most breathtaking sequences ever filmed in a vampire movie. After Van Helsing locates Dracula's lair, the vampire flees to his castle with his future mistress. Naturally, the battle between good and evil is staged in Castle Dracula, where Van Helsing and the Count feverishly battle each other to the finish. Van Helsing forces the vampire into the sun's early morning rays with a crucifix fabricated from two candlesticks. Like a laser beam, the rays rip right through the flesh of the vampire, who painfully decomposes into a pile of dust. As a result of the fast-paced graphic action, HORROR OF DRACULA was an immediate success world-wide and rolled-in handsome profits for Hammer Studios. The film launched a long series of Dracula films with Christopher Lee as Dracula and reshaped the face of the horror film forever. HORROR OF DRACULA is a masterpiece of horror and perhaps one of the best Dracula and vampire films ever made and undeniably one of cinema's most influential films.

THE UNEARTHLY

Universal   1959

A young cowboy named Drake Roby is hired by the film's heroine and cowgirl to hunt down the man responsible for killing her father and brother. Little does she know Drake is a vampire who drinks the warm blood of humans. The vampirized gunslinger helps out the young girl, but finds himself falling in love with her. He then puts her under his spell and drinks her blood until a local preacher realizes that he is a vampire and kills him with a silver crucifix. The film was the first to feature a vampire in the wild, wild west, but certainly not the last.

BRIDES OF DRACULA

Hammer   1960

Next to HORROR OF DRACULA, BRIDES OF DRACULA is perhaps Hammer's greatest film from the studio's earlier days. One word describes this vampire film: Brilliant! The screenplay by Jimmy Sangster is well conceived and Terence Fisher's stylish direction creates a strong mood of Gothic horror. Christopher Lee was originally intended to return to the role of Count Dracula while Peter Cushing was asked to reprise his Professor Van Helsing role. However, Lee was unable to don the cloak so soon in his career after appearing in CURSE OF FRANKENSTEIN (1957), HORROR OF DRACULA (1958) and THE MUMMY (1959) in fear that he would become typecast as a horror actor. As a result of Lee's decision, Sangster had to redraft the script; thus actor David Peel was cast in the place of Christopher Lee, but not as Count Dracula. Instead, Peel portrayed Baron Meinster, a very devious, sinister and cunning vampire. Peel was about forty years old at the time the film was made, but Hammer's chief make-up artist Roy Ashton transformed the middle-aged actor into a handsome blonde, boyish-looking vampire. Because neither Dracula nor his brides appear in this film, the title is thus misleading, but Sangster, to avoid lack of continuity, has added a narrative read by the voice of Peter Cushing during the film's prologue explaining that Baron Meinster is simply one of Dracula's many disciples. The film offers dramatic confrontations between Professor Van Helsing and Baron Meinster, an incestuous sub-plot between Meinster and his Baroness mother (brilliantly played by Martita Hunt), and another great Hammer climax, in which the vampire is destroyed symbolically when he happens across the shadow of a gigantic cross cast from the reflection of a windmill vane against the moonlight. This dynamic and enthusiastic film is well crafted and is regarded by film historians as a modern horror classic.

BLACK SUNDAY

AIP   1960

The German title for this Italian horror

film was THE HOUR WHEN DRACULA COMES. The film was known as THE MASK OF THE DEMON in Italy and in England as REVENGE OF THE VAMPIRE. BLACK SUNDAY was director Mario Bava's debut as a filmmaker, and what a frightening film he produced. Though not really a Dracula film, BLACK SUNDAY stars horror starlet Barbara Steele in the dual role of an evil vampire witch named Princess Asa and her mortal descendant Katya. Asa is found guilty of vampirism and witchcraft and as her sentence, she is bound to a large cross and executed by a spiked mask which is pounded into her face. The Dracula character in the film (in which the German distributor derived its title from) is apparently her lover Prince Javutich (Arturo Dominici), whose appearance resembles that of many screen Draculas, primarily that of Chris Lee's. The prince is given the same grisly death. But before Asa dies she swears she will return from the grave for vengeance, and she does! That is, centuries later when a doctor and his assistant inadvertently splatter the blood of a huge bat over the ashes of her corpse. It is now Black Sunday, the day Satan walks the Earth every hundred years, and the prince of a nearby castle fears that his ancestor might return from the grave. Asa, now fully revived, summons her Prince Javutich to rise, and together they plan to destroy their ancestors. However, Asa has plans of her own which include taking the place of Katya, whose physically identical. Nobody would ever know! In a fierce battle, the young doctor who inadvertently revived Asa kills the prince first, but when he reaches the tomb of Asa he finds two identical women claiming to be Katya. The doctor is mistakenly about to impale the real Katya with a wooden shaft when he notices her crucifix. Realizing he's about to kill the wrong person, he pulls Asa's cloak away revealing the rotting ribs of a corpse. The rotting vampiress is taken away by the villagers and burned at the stake and damned to an eternal death. BLACK SUNDAY is certainly of Italy's most supreme horror films and Bava's

Gothic atmosphere is stunning, as he uses darkness and shadows to create the uneasy mood of fear and horror.

THE WORLD OF THE VAMPIRE
Cinematografica   1960

Apparently producer Abel Salazar and his film company Cinematografica was very busy making vampire films during the late 1950's and 1960's. In this film directed by veteran filmmaker Alfonso Corona Blake, a vampire named Count Subotay rules over a horde of cloaked vampires who reside beneath an old house. Subotay uses a large pipe organ composed of human bones to control his cult of vampires with whom he plans to use to exterminate mankind. The vampires are destroyed when the film's hero plays a specialized music on Subotay's organ while the central vampire figure is destroyed in a fierce battle with the hero and pushed into a pit of stakes. Despite the bizarre plot, the film was perhaps one of Mexico's better vampire movies, that is, in terms of atmosphere and photography.

THE VAMPIRE'S LAST VICTIM
Nord Film   1960

Released in the United States as THE PLAYGIRLS AND THE VAMPIRE, this Italian-made film directed by Piero Regnoli stars Walter Brandi in a dual role as Count Gabor Kernassy and his twin brother who just happens to be a vampire. When a group of sexy show girls stay the night at Castle Kernassy, the vampirized brother makes his moves. The film plays more towards its sexual content rather than toward serious horror. THE VAMPIRE'S LAST VICTIM is not a film that would please the masses of horror and vampire film enthusiasts, but admirers of pornographic films should be pleased.

CRY OF THE VAMPIRE
Pao International   1960

This Italian-made vampire film features a handsome and distinguished looking Baron who preys on fine Italian women during the night hours. The vampire figure is made up to look much like Christopher Lee's Dracula and he

also perishes much like Lee's vampire in HORROR OF DRACULA (1958). The film is directed with atmospheric beauty by Theodora Fec.

BLOOD AND ROSES
E.G.E. Films (Italian)   1960

Roger Vadim directs this elegant and slow-moving tale of lesbian vampirism based on the novel Carmilla by Sheridan Le Fanu. As Carmilla Von Karnstein is Vadim's beautiful blonde wife Annette Vadim. In the film, Carmilla is possessed by the spirit of a long-entombed vampire. Carmilla seduces Georgia Monteverdi (Elsa Martinelli), slowly draining the young girl's blood until one day, returning to her grave, the vampire inadvertently stumbles upon a wooden shaft that destroys her. This was the first time that a vampire killed itself, weather intentional or unintentional. Vadim's version of the Le Fanu story is blatant in its lesbian elements, but the film does offer some good dream sequences and strong atmospheric photography. BLOOD AND ROSES was the first screen adaptation of the Le Fanu novel since Carl Dreyer's VAMPYR (1932).

THE CURSE OF NOSTRADAMUS
Cinematografica   1960

Actor German Robles returns to the screen as Mexico's newest vampire sensation, Nostradamus! Roble's new vampire is cloaked all in black with a Satanic mustache and beard. As Nostradamus, he is totally evil and ruthless in his attempt to establish a vampire cult. He is established as a creature who must sleep in his coffin containing the ashes of his ancestors. Only bullets made of platinum can destroy him. The low budget film tells how Nostradamus threatens the film's savant Dr. Dolan (Domingo Soler) by telling him that he will claim the lives of thirteen unlucky people unless he cooperates. Nostradamus's plans are temporarily halted when he is trapped in a tunnel cave-in. Sounds exciting? Anyway, the first film in the " Nostradamus" series, as with all the entries, was produced on a shoe-string budget and from scripts that lacked any imagination or originality (obviously)!

NOSTRADAMUS AND THE DESTROYER OF MONSTERS

Cinematografica 1960

Made immediately after production on the first film was completed, this sequel, also directed by Frederick Curiel, tells how the vampire Nostradamus (German Robles) returns from his previous entrapment to enslave a condemned murderer to assist in his revenge against Dr. Dolan. The good-hearted doctor develops an electronic device that uses sound waves to torment vampire bats and kill human vampires.

NOSTRADAMUS, THE GENIUS FROM THE DARK

Cinematografica 1960

In this, the third installment in the four film series involving the vampire Nostradamus, the vampire's ashes from his coffin are scattered in the wind when Dr. Dolan and a group of villagers storm his tomb. This segment in the series is not nearly as good as the previous films, which is not really saying much for this movie!

THE BLOOD OF NOSTRADAMUS

Cinematografica 1961

Considered the best (if you can believe?) and the last of the Nostradamus films made within a two year period, THE BLOOD OF NOSTRADAMUS reveals to us that the famous vampire substituted his ancestral ashes in his coffin with the ashes of his victims. The ruthless vampire is eventually chased by police and destroyed forever with the timeless stake through the heart. Thus concludes the series of the legendary Mexican vampire Nostradamus. This film is also directed by Frederick Curiel.

ATOM AGE VAMPIRE

Lion 1961

Also released under the unfamiliar title of SEDDOK, this Italian-made low budget science fiction horror film features a scientist (Alberto Lupo) who undergoes tissue transplants that transform him into a hideous beast that requires human blood to maintain his existence. The film, directed by Richard McNamara, is actually one of the better combinations of science fiction and vampirism from the 1960's.

FRANKENSTEIN, THE VAMPIRO AND COMPANY

Cinematografica 1961

This Mexican remake of Universal's ABBOTT AND COSTELLO MEET FRANKENSTEIN (1948) is directed by Benito Alazraki. Unlike the Abbott and Costello picture, the vampire of this film is never really referred to as Dracula. The plot is quite simple and feeble. Two wax figures of the Vampire and the Frankenstein Monster are assigned to an express agency in the care of comedians Paco and Agapito. They are employed to deliver the wax figures to a spooky old mansion where the wax figures actually come to life. The Vampire has plans of giving the Frankenstein Monster the brain of Agapito and then use the Monster to conquer America. The unexplained appearance of the Wolfman interrupts the operation, and both the werewolf and the Vampire battle each other until they are destroyed in a fire. The Frankenstein Monster is left to sink in a bog. Sounds familiar? Quite!

THE VAMPIRE OF THE OPERA

NIF 1961

Renato Polselli directed this Italian-made vampire film about a vampire (Giuseppe Addobati) who is devoted to the opera. The film, set in and around an opera house, is a combination of DRACULA and THE PHANTOM OF THE OPERA. The vampire uses a ghost to warn a theatrical group at the opera house, but when they do not take the warning serious, the vampire begins attending rehearsals and attacking various performers. The vampire is eventually trapped upon the stage and set ablaze by the performers.

THE VAMPIRE'S LOVER

CIF 1961

Better known as THE VAMPIRE AND THE BALLERINA, this film tells how two female members caught in a rainstorm are forced to stay the night in a castle inhabited by two vampires, the Contessa (Maria Luisa Rolando) and her cloaked servant (Iscaro Ravajoli). The Contessa sends her servant to drink the blood of her female guests. She then oddly drinks the blood from the neck of her servant, which is a strange diversion from the traditional method. As she drains off his stolen blood, her servant reverts to a withered old man. Inspired by the climax of HORROR OF DRACULA (1958), the film's hero forms a cross from two candlesticks and drives the vampires into the burning sunlight. the film was atmospherically directed by Renato Polselli.

THE BAD FLOWER

Sun Glim Film 1961

This Korean remake of the classic Hammer Dracula film HORROR OF DRACULA (1958) stars Chimi Kim as Dracula and Yechoon Lee as Van Helsing, Korean style. The film was directed by Yongmin Lee and blends Oriental mysticism with the Dracula legend.

THE BLOODY VAMPIRE

Tele-Talia 1961

A very atmospheric Mexican production that often resembles the cinematic work of famous Italian filmmaker Mario Bava. The film begins very promising, with a cloaked skeleton driving a coach through the fog in slow motion. Unfortunately, the story and atmosphere is not consistent with the opening reel as Count Frankenhausen (Carlos Agosti) rises from his coffin-like trunk and goes to great length to transform his wife into a vampire. The film was poorly written and directed by Miguel Morayta and, if you can believe, actually influenced a sequel entitled THE INVASION OF THE VAMPIRES (1962).

SANTO VS. THE VAMPIRE WOMEN

Corona Panamericana   1961

During the 1960's, Mexico produced several vampire and horror films in which wrestlers were depicted as heroes. The most popular of the Mexican masked wrestlers and super-heroes was Santo, and in this "famous" Mexican film directed by Alfonso Corona Blake, Santo must wrestle several masked vampires in the ring. In one memorable and ridiculous scene which is actually the film's highlight, Santo unmasks one of his opponents to reveal the face of a snarling werewolf! The monster then transforms into a bat a flies away. During the climax of the film, Santo battles several male vampires, keeping them occupied until the sun rises and incinerates them to dust, which is what should happen to this film: incinerate to dust!

UNCLE WAS A VAMPIRE

Embassy 1961

Originally produced and released in Italy in 1959 by Maxima as HARD TIME FOR VAMPIRES, UNCLE WAS A VAMPIRE features the talents of Christopher Lee as a fanged and cloaked Count Dracula-like vampire named Baron Rodriguez. Lee's vampiric Baron is actually a spoof on his own Count Dracula characterization, and although the film is basically a comedy, Lee maintains a serious portrayal of his vampire, much along the lines of Bela Lugosi's Dracula characterization in ABBOTT AND COSTELLO MEET FRANKENSTEIN (1948).   The film showcases the cinematography of Marco Scarpelli and the stylish direction of Stefano Steno, both resulting in some fine, atmospheric vampire footage of Chris Lee prowling the rooftops of his castle with his cape majestically flowing in the wind. Despite the low production values (in comparison to Hammer vampire films), director Steno does a great job combining horror with comedy. In the film, Baron Oswald (played by Italy's top comedian at the time, Renato Rascel) looses his fortune and is forced to sell his castle. To the Baron's dismay, the castle is turned into a hotel, and he is forced to take a job as a bellboy.   Baron Rodriguez arrives on the scene and begins attacking the women guests at the hotel, resulting in chaos and panic in the Gothic structure.

INVASION OF THE VAMPIRES

Tela-Talia   1962

Sequel to THE BLOODY VAMPIRE (1960) in which Count Frankenhausen (Carlos Agosti) returns with plans of invading the world (AGAIN?) with an army of vampires under his royal command. A Van Helsing-like scientist opposes the vampire with a mysterious flower from a plant called the Mandagora. The plant itself has toxic effects on the undead. The Count is staked and destroyed in his bat form and all of his victims return to their original life form and live happily ever after.

SLAUGHTER   OF   THE VAMPIRES

CIF   1962

Italy does it again with this new version of DRACULA (1931) and HORROR OF DRACULA (1958) written and directed by Roberto Mauri.   Two vampires, one resembling Dracula and the other his bride, are pursued by angry villagers.   The vampiress is impaled by a pitchfork, but the Dracula-like vampire escapes. The film then proceeds to tell how the vampire begins making advances towards a new woman, who one day becomes one of the undead too.   Her husband seeks the aide of a Van Helsing-type vampire killer and together they hunt the fiend responsible down.   The vampire is killed when the spikes of an iron gate penetrate his chest.

KISS OF THE VAMPIRE

Hammer   1963

KISS OF THE VAMPIRE, ironically Hammer's most superior vampire tale, was unfortunately a failure at the box office in comparison to Hammer's HORROR OF DRACULA (1958) and BRIDES OF DRACULA (1960). The reasons for its failure are quite simple. To begin with, the film lacked the key personalities of, say Christopher Lee or Peter Cushing.   Secondly, KISS OF THE VAMPIRE is a more subtitle and artistic vampire film, which, right from the start, eliminates the half of the horror movie fans who only want to see blood and violence straight from the beginning. Finally, the vampires in this film are not exactly the most dynamic species. Instead, they are very subtitle about their identities and their nocturnal practices. Amazingly, the script, written by John Elder, is one of the finest vampire tales ever written. But because director Don Sharp does not have the knack and enthusiasm that Terence Fisher would have incorporated into this fantastic story, KISS OF THE VAMPIRE. Needless to say, the film is evenly paced and the story is quite interesting.   A honeymooning couple (Edward de Souza and Jennifer Daniel) encounter a vampire cult headed by a noble Count Ravna (played in a restrained fashion by Noel Willman). The Count invites the couple to his chateau, where they soon discover that their host is a vampire. There is an elegant and fascinating masked ball for the vampires, and the vampire cult's destruction by vicious vampire bats is quite good. Willman's vampire, not as dynamic as Chris Lee's Dracula, is, if anything, convincing and Clifford Evan's vampire killer and the film's defined savant is actually superb and, at times, superior to Peter Cushing's performances as Van Helsing. The lavish sets of Bernard Robinson are fabulous. It is a shame that American audiences have not been privileged to the superior uncut version that circulated throughout British theaters. KISS OF THE VAMPIRE was released in America as KISS OF EVIL.

TERROR IN THE CRYPT

Hispaner Films (Spain) 1963

A faithful screen adaptation of Sheridan Le Fanu's Carmilla , which Christopher Lee portrays Count Ludwig Karnstein. In the film, Count Ludwig's evil housekeeper summons the spirit of a vampiress who was executed centuries ago.   The blond vampiress slowly takes revenge on the Karnstein family until she is eventually staked in her crypt. The film is often dull in its direction by Camillo Mastrocinque, but the black and white photography of Julion Ortas is quite impressive. Much better is Roger Vadim's BLOOD AND ROSES (1960). TERROR IN THE CRYPT was released in Spain as THE CURSE OF THE KARNSTEINS.

PLANET OF THE VAMPIRES
AIP   1965

The first full blown science fiction-vampire film in which an expedition crew maneuver their spacecraft to the distant planet of Aura where they themselves are transformed into vampirized zombies. The Auranians plan to sabotage the American spacecraft and leave their dying planet for Earth, where they will rule supremely. The vampiric aliens manage to escape during the film's climax, which was probably AIP's idea of leaving possibilities open for a sequel should this film take-off at the box office. The film is atmospherically directed by Mario Bava, but unfortunately, PLANET OF THE VAMPIRES did not take off as planned and quickly faded from the box office scene.

DRACULA - PRINCE OF DARKNESS
Hammer   1965

Originally conceived under its preliminary title DRACULA'S REVENGE (which would have been an appropriate title since the Hammer Dracula films from here on end would usually base its premise mostly upon the theme of revenge), DRACULA - PRINCE OF DARKNESS is actually a very good, well mounted vampire film. Yes the film has several if not many flaws, but the overall production is quite clever and original, as written by Jimmy Sangster. Christopher Lee returns to the role of Count Dracula, however, by the making of this film, the actor had become a high paid star, and the studio could not afford to have Lee deliver the meaty dialogue written

for him by Sangster. As a result, the screen treatment was entirely redrafted in which all of the vampire's dialogue was eliminated from the script; thus you have Chris Lee's Dracula emerging from shadows to hiss and bare his fangs at his victims. This disappointed fans, but when one views the film today, the lack of dialogue just does not hinder the film. Jimmy Sangster did not see it that way. Outraged, Sangster removed his name from the credits and replaced it with the fictitious name of John Sansom. One wonders how much greater a film DRACULA - PRINCE OF DARKNESS would have been had Lee delivered the lines originally written for him. Director Terence Fisher opens the film with footage of Dracula's memorable destruction from the climax of HORROR OF DRACULA. Now that continuity has been established, the film proceeds to tell a new story. Four travelers inadvertently arrive at Castle Dracula. One of the couples fall prey to the vampire. The husband is destroyed and his blood is used to revive Dracula, while the wife (played by Barbara Shelley) is transformed into Dracula's evil vampire mistress. Together, Dracula and his new mistress torture the lives of the other couple (Francis Matthews and Suzan Farmer), the latter becomes Dracula's next intended bride. The climax is most brilliant. Dracula is dramatically destroyed when he becomes trapped beneath the layers of ice that surround his castle. The Sangster script also introduces a new addition to the vampire folklore proclaiming that a vampire cannot cross running water and that running water can actually destroy a vampire upon contact. Fisher also makes use of the well constructed, spacious sets, since most of this film is staged within the castle walls of Castle Dracula. This is a good example of how Hammer's technique of making relatively low budget films appear expensive, and in this respect, that is what makes DRACULA-PRINCE OF DARKNESS so grand, despite its numerous but minuscule flaws.

SANTO VS. BARON BRAKULA
Vagara   1965

Santo - the masked wrestler returns to battle vampire Baron Brakula in this film labeled as a Mexican remake of Hammer's HORROR OF DRACULA (1958) with Santo substituting as Van Helsing. Brakula attacks a female victim, who is saved with blood transfusions. The vampire, grinning with bloody fangs, reclaims his victim, and digs a grave for her, until Santo arrives on the scene and the two nemesis engage in a fierce battle. I'm sure Hammer Studios loved the producers of the film!

BILLY THE KID VS. DRACULA
Embassy   1966

Actor John Carradine won the part of Count Dracula in this ludicrous vehicle directed by William Beaudine, a veteran director of " B" westerns. However, although the film was produced on a very low budget, director Beaudine does manage to deliver a good old-fashion cowboy film marketed towards Saturday kiddie matinees. Naturally, Dracula is the villain, who begins his prey by attacking a young Indian girl and then massacres the occupants of a stagecoach, assuming the identity of one of his victims. He then sets his sights after the film's heroine (Melinda Plowman), but Billy the Kid (Chuck Courtney), now turned hero, destroys the vampire with a surgeon's scalpel, reducing Dracula to dust. Carradine, now older, has the ability to transform into a vampire bat as in his former Dracula films and his vampire cast no image in a mirror; however, the film does have many flaws, one of which are the scenes in which the vampire is seen parading around in the light, an obvious oversight on behalf of the director - I'm sure. These oversights are to be expected from such a low budget feature, I guess.

THE EMPIRE OF DRACULA
Filmica   1966

Also known as THE WOMEN OF DRACULA, this Mexican-made vampire film portrays Count Dracula as a handsome and dynamic figure as played by Lucha Villa. Dracula, surrounded by beautiful vampire women, terrorizes the Mexican countryside, leaping onto moving carriages and attacking unsuspecting victims. The film does have lesbian aspects in which women are bitten by female vampires and several dramatic moments such as when the fanged vampire is fought in his coffin by a man wielding a crucifix. Mexico was famous for producing some very fast paced and action packed vampire films, and this one is, without a doubt, certainly one of those.

DR. TERROR'S GALLERY OF HORRORS
American General   1966

Made to capitalize on the very successful anthology horror films made in Great Britain, DR. TERROR'S GALLERY OF HORRORS is comprised of five short segments of horror. Two of the five segments are vampire tales. The first is entitled King Vampire, in which a vampire in nineteenth century London is revealed to be the female secretary of the police inspector investigating the case. The other segment was entitled Count Alucard. The title role was originally intended for John Carradine, who had other commitments at the time. Therefore the role went to actor Mitch Evans. The tale adheres to the opening chapters of Bram Stoker's Dracula with Jonathan Harker journeying to Castle Alucard to sell him the carfax property in London. Evans delivers the expected dialogue, and Harker is attacked by a female vampire, who is destroyed by angry villagers. Harker returns to castle Alucard and accuses the Count of being a vampire. At that moment, Harker unexpectedly transforms into a werewolf and kills the vampire king. DR. TERROR'S GALLERY OF HORRORS is amateurishly directed by David Hewitt and is inferior to other horror anthology films made during that time, the better of which were made by Amicus Film Company.

QUEEN OF BLOOD
AIP   1966

This offbeat tale combines science fiction with horror as a space expedition from Earth arrives near the planet of Mars. The crew invite the Queen of Mars onto their spacecraft. We later find out that she is indeed the Queen of Blood that the title suggests as she seduces the crew one by one and drains them intimately of their blood. After killing off most of the crew, she engages in a battle with one of the remaining survivors and accidentally cuts herself during the struggle. Since the vampiress is a hemophiliac by nature, she slowly bleeds to her death. The bizarre film is directed by Curtis Harrington and is considered a cult classic among fans of horror films. It is undoubtedly one of the most unusual of these films.

TOWER OF THE DEVIL
Hemisphere   1966

Directed by Lauro Pacheo, this bizarre Philippine-made film concerns a cult of vampires who attempt to get a strange pregnant woman, who actually sucks the blood of lizards, to give birth to their vampire offspring. The leader of the vampire cult (played by Ramon D'Salva) leads his cult of fellow vamps in an attack against some nasty werewolves. The monsters are all destroyed at the mercy of an earthquake. But the lizard-blood sucking woman's offspring carries on the heritage. Good God. Who writes these ridiculous films?

HERCULES IN THE HAUNTED WORLD
Omnia   1966

Christopher Lee plays Lico the vampire in this Italian epic directed by the great Italian filmmaker Mario Bava. Lico requires the blood of a beautiful princess to become immortal. Hercules (Red Park) learns that he can save the princess by obtaining a certain mystical plant located deep in the pits of Hell. Once there, he must overcome flying vampires and other creatures, which eventually lead him to the climatic battle with Lico, who is pinned under a boulder and left to

perishes when the sun emerges after a lunar eclipse. The film offers great sets, and strong atmospheric direction by Bava and is perhaps one of the better Italian-made musclemen films from the 1960's.

A TASTE OF BLOOD
Creative Film Enterprise   1966

Producer, director Herschell Gordon Lewis is notorious for producing some of the most gruesome horror films from the 1960's and 1970's. TASTE OF BLOOD was his sole effort into the vampire genre. A man (played by Bill Rogers) receives a mysterious package from Yugoslavia containing rare brandy. The liquid causes the man to become nocturnal, sleeping by day and prowling about at night. In visiting his mother country, the man discovers that he is a descendant of Count Dracula and that the brandy was actually his ancestor's blood. The man returns to America as a full-fledged vampire and is eventually destroyed in his coffin by Dr. Howard Helsing (Otto Schlesinger), but not after some very graphic stakings, mutilations and gory violence - Lewis style.

THE VAMPIRE GIRLS
Filmica Vergara   1967

John Carradine returns to the role of Count Dracula (again!) in this Mexican-made film directed by Federico Curiel. Dracula (Carradine) is imprisoned behind bars, and his Countess must take over and command a cult of vampire women in an attempt to free her hubby. The film's hero is one of Mexico's famous masked wrestlers " Thousand Masks," who enters the vampire's castle and battles her muscular henchmen and her vampire minions outfitted in tights and ridiculous capped-winged cloaks.

DANCE OF THE VAMPIRES
MGM   1967

Also known as THE FEARLESS VAMPIRE KILLERS and PARDON ME, BUT YOUR TEETH ARE IN MY NECK, DANCE OF THE VAMPIRE is perhaps one of the better vampire films ever made, which is ironic because the film is a spoof on the vampire genre directed by Roman Polanski and tells the story of a Professor Van Helsing-type vampire hunter who sets out to investigate rumors of a community of vampires in Transylvania. The film offers strong atmosphere, larger than life settings, clever plot twists and good performances despite the comedy elements. It is a shame that American prints of the film were drastically re-edited.

SPACE VAMPIRES (1969)

Gemini   1968

A far from terrifying tale about corpse stealers, bug-eyed outer space vampire-monsters, mutant brutes and human transplants with actor John Carradine in one of his worst performances. Even the FBI and special agents from Chinese government are involved. This ludicrous horror-sci-fi mish mash is also known as ASTRO ZOMBIES.

DRACULA HAS RISEN FROM THE GRAVE

HAMMER   1968

Perhaps the most underrated of the Hammer-Dracula films. Christopher Lee returns as Count Dracula! This time, he delivers dialogue in the form of authoritative commands, which, I suppose, is better than no dialogue. Director Freddie Francis makes great use of the bumped-up budget, resulting in a larger than life vampire epic. Francis uses heavy religious symbolism to create a defined line between good and evil. The premise, based on the familiar theme of revenge, is well written by John Elder (producer Anthony Hind's writing name). The film begins when Dracula is miraculously released from the icy prison that once held him captive during the climax of the previous film. However, now free, Dracula cannot enter his castle because it has been exorcised by a powerful Monsignor. Enraged, the vampire uses a weak-willed Priest (Ewan Hooper) to locate the Monsignor's family, and then the killing begins. Dracula uses his uncontrollable quench for blood to

destroy the family, eventually setting his site on the niece (played by the lovely Veronica Carlson). In the film, Dracula meets several near deaths, including a spectacular sequence in which he is caught slumbering in his coffin by the Priest, who has temporarily escaped Dracula's powers, and the film's hero, Paul (Barry Andrews). As the sun begins to set, they ram a wooden stake through Dracula's heart, but the fiend jumps out of his coffin and painfully removes the stake from his own chest and fires it like a missile at Paul and then escapes to his castle. For this scene, Hammer added a bit of their own folklore in which certain religious prayers were required to destroy the vampire eternally. Since Paul is portrayed as an atheist in the film and the Priest is still under the Satanic influence of Dracula, their were no prayers and the vampire was able to remove the stake and escape. An action-packed chase scene follows in which Dracula and Paul battle each other on the front terrace of Castle Dracula. The vampire is inadvertently tossed over the terrace where he is impaled by the crucifix below. In a desperate attempt to destroy the vampire, the Priest regains his faith in God and delivers the words of exorcism that send the vampire king to the here-after. DRACULA HAS RISEN FROM THE GRAVE is visually stunning and features some fabulous rooftops sets by Bernard Robinson. The cast is excellent, especially Ewan Hooper as the enslaved Priest and the music score by James Bernard is quite compelling.

THE MARK OF THE WOLFMAN

Maxpar   1968

This Spanish-made horror film was the beginning of a series of werewolf movies starring Paul Naschy. The series occasionally featured various vampires, including Count Dracula himself. MARK OF THE WOLFMAN was released in Asia as THE WOLFMAN OF COUNT DRACULA and in Germany as THE WOLFMAN...THE VAMPIRE OF DR. DRACULA, while in Belgium the film

was known as DRACULA AND THE WEREWOLF. The film was released in the United States under the very misleading title FRANKENSTEIN'S BLOODY TERROR by Independent International. The film never really features Dracula by name, nor does it feature any relatives to the Frankenstein's. However there is a vampire named Dr. Mikelhov whose mannerisms resemble that of Count Dracula's. In any event, this rich atmospheric film directed by E.L. Eguiluz begins when two gypsies loot the resting place of a man with a silver cross imbedded in his heart. The two greedy men remove the shimmering object only to die at the fangs of a savage werewolf. Later, young Waldemar Daninsky (Paul Naschy) joins the villagers in a search for his werewolf-father and he is attacked by the beast, killing it with the silver dagger. Now Waldemar has inherited the curse and now he transforms into the dreaded beast when the moon is full. Both his girlfriend and best friend chain him to the castle cellar and send for a mysterious Dr. Mikelhov, who happens to be a vampire. The vampire deceives the young couple into thinking that he will cure Waldemar of his inherited curse, but in actuality, he has plans of using the powers of the Devil to make the beast even stronger. In a motion picture first, the werewolf escapes from the cellar and battles it out with the vampire, who bursts into flames. Waldemar is eventually shot with a silver bullet, but have no fear, for the famous Spanish werewolf returns in the sequel to this film! Despite the comic book style in which the film is presented, MARK OF THE WEREWOLF is extremely atmospheric and a very exciting entry in the vampire genre.

SANTO AND THE TREASURE OF DRACULA

Calderon   1968

Santo goes back in time in a scientific device which allows him to locate Count Dracula, whose running around Mexico, or somewhere, incognito as Count Alucard. The vampire is

21

destroyed by a wooden stake through the heart, and Santo journeys back to the present to locate Dracula's grave to steal the nobleman's royal ring, which is considered very valuable. Villains remove the stake from the fiend's heart, and once again, Santo must battle the undead, this time in the present. The film ends with another timeless stake driven through Count Dracula's heart. SANTO AND THE TREASURE OF DRACULA is directed by Rene Cardona and features mindless sex and nude chorus girls to appeal to an adult market. The film did poorly at the box office. Are you surprised?

TASTE THE BLOOD OF DRACULA

Hammer   1969

Another underrated Dracula epic from Hammer. This film brilliantly captures the Victorian period in costume and sets, and I must say, much more effectively than Universal's DRACULA (1979). The John Elder screenplay, though a bit confusing because of poor editing, is perhaps the most interesting of the Hammer films. Three wealthy businessmen are taken in by an evil disciple of Satan and Count Dracula. With the financial support of the three businessmen, the evil disciple (Ralph Bates) inadvertently resurrects Count Dracula from the hereafter. From this point forward, Dracula (played by Christopher Lee) takes revenge against the families of the three men responsible for killing his loyal disciple. One wonders why Dracula wastes his time killing the men who actually helped revived him instead of going after the people responsible for killing him in DRACULA HAS RISEN FROM THE GRAVE. To me, this is where the film's motivation becomes a bit misplaced. In any event, Dracula succeeds in killing everyone off except the film's heroine, who he takes to his hideout in a desecrated church. There, the film's hero battles with the Count and because of his faith in God, all holiness is restored to the church and its religious symbols, causing the vampire

to fall to his death on the alter below. The powers of goodness prevail over evil once more, and this is what the Hammer films usually based their premises on: Good against evil. TASTE THE BLOOD OF DRACULA was Peter Sasdy's directorial debut, and although there are problems with the script, Sasdy has turned out a colorful and exciting effort that unfortunately continues to go underrated. Sasdy projects his Dracula as a ruthless beast who destroys the children of the businessmen first before killing off each of the men. The film is a portrait in horror pitted against a Victorian setting with strong atmosphere and mood. Despite the weak editing of this film, TASTE THE BLOOD OF DRACULA remains very satisfying in an authentic kind of way.

BLOOD OF DRACULA'S CASTLE

Crown International   1969

Producer Al Adamson's film is perhaps one of the worst vampire films ever made. In fact, I would go as far as to say that BLOOD OF DRACULA'S CASTLE is one of the worst horror films ever made. Well, maybe not the worst, but definitely among the top five! The film suffers from weak scripting and from low production values resulting in poor sets and horrid performances by its cast. Poor John Carradine stars not as Dracula, but as the vampire's murderous butler. The actor is totally wasted in what is probably one of his worst performances. Count Dracula is portrayed here by Alex D'Arcy. In the film, Dracula and his Countess (played by Paula Raymond) attempt to conceal their identities by changing their names to Alucard (AGAIN!). They sleep in coffins in their bedrooms and drink human blood from cocktail glasses. In the cellar below are young maidens whom Carradine taps for blood. To make matters more confusing, an escape convict arrives to the castle and causes mayhem when he transforms into a werewolf. Sound like one of those horrible Santo Vs. the monster(s) movies. The Draculas are

destroyed by the sun's rays during the film's climax, but two bat like creatures rise from the ashes to suggest that they survive. Producer Adamson announced a sequel entitled DRACULA'S COFFIN that was never made: Thank God!

SANTO AND THE BLUE DEMON VS. THE MONSTERS

Cinematografica   1969

Famous Mexican wrestler Santo teams up with another popular Mexican wrestler to do battle with a horde of monsters headed by The Vampire (David Alvizu). Together with his vampirized bride, The Vampire joins forces with Mexico's version of the Frankenstein Monster, the Wolfman, the Mummy, and the Cyclops to battle the masked heroes. The poorly made film is directed by Gilberto Martinez.

SANTO AND THE BLUE DEMON VS. DRACULA AND THE WOLFMAN

Calderon   1968

Side by side once again are Santo and the Blue Demon bringing justice to the world of the undead. In this vehicle, Dracula is revived when human blood splatters into his coffin and onto his ashy remains. Both Dracula and the Wolfman go after friends of Santo and the Blue Demon. Throughout the course of the film, Dracula manages to create a horde of vampire women and the Wolfman creates a horde of other werewolves to spice up the entertainment level (for juveniles). The filmmakers have a field day making the climax of this picture with our heroes fighting all the vampires and werewolves and throwing them into a pit of stakes. Dracula and the Wolfman suffer the same doom. The color film is directed by Miguel M. Delgado much in the same style as the previous Santo films.

DRAKULITA

RJF Productions   1969

Direct from the isle of the Philippines, this tale of vampirism is directed by Consuelo P. Osorio and stars actress Rossana Ortiz as a female vampire known as Drakulita, who terrorizes the comedic cast trapped in an old dark house! This film cannot be that great if I am able to describe it in its entirety all in one sentence. Judge for yourself.

DRACULA - THE DIRTY OLD MAN

Boyd Productions   1969

Made in Dripping color, this film was originally planned as a sex film but producer, writer and director William Edwards eventually realized that by way of proper editing, this film could become a good comedy. The film offers bizarre and offbeat characters and Dracula, once again under the synonym of Alucard, is portrayed as a dirty old man by Vince Kelly. In the film, Alucard goes around seducing young girls, quarreling with his mother (literally an old bat) and hypnotizing a man into becoming a werewolf. In short, the film is a fiasco.

THE MAN WHO CAME FROM UMMO

Eichberg Film   1970

Directed by Tulio Demicheli, this Spanish, Italian and West German co-production is established as a true Dracula film with a twist, starring Paul Naschy as both the werewolf Waldemar Daninsky and the Frankenstein Monster. Actor Michael Rennie plays a scientist from the distant planet Ummo. In this film, the alien scientist arrives on planet Earth with intentions of conquering the entire Universe. To do this, he enlists the aide of the four most infamous monsters of history and revives Count Dracula, the werewolf, the Frankenstein Monster and the mummy. The alien's mad plot is halted by secret agent Craig Hill, and so is this ridiculous Naschy epic. This is perhaps one of the actor's worse efforts.

CURSE OF THE VAMPIRES

Hemisphere   1970

Released on a double bill with Hemisphere's BEAST OF BLOOD (1970), CURSE OF THE VAMPIRES takes place at the turn of the century.

Amelia Fuentis and Eddie Garcia play brother and sister. They return to their father's hacienda in a small island town in the Philippines. They find their father sick and tormented, and discover that their mother, whom they had supposed dead, is being held prisoner by their father in the basement of their mansion because she is a vampire. Eddie tries to visit his mother one evening; she attacks him, turning him into a vampire too. He goes to his sweetheart and turns her into a vampire. Now there are three vampires to stake instead of one. Eventually, the father goes after his wife and drives a wooden stake through her heart, relieving her of her misery. Now Eddie kills his father, but Amelia's boyfriend's father tries to kill Eddie and his girlfriend (the latter is his daughter) by driving a wooden stake through their hearts. He does so, but the ghosts of the mother and Eddie frightens his horse and kills him.   Did you get all that?   This mish-mash of plot twists that involves vampires and spectres is directed Gerardo De Leon from a confusing script written by Ben Faleo and Pierre L. Salas. Claimed to have been filmed in "The real tombs of horror!"- whatever that means?

THE   NIGHT   OF   THE WALPURGIS

Plata Films   1970

Paul Naschy had just completed two werewolf films (NIGHT OF THE WOLFMAN and THE FURY OF THE WOLFMAN) and was cast to star in this new werewolf epic for director Leon Klimovsky. Although the film was released in France as THE CLAWS OF DRACULA, the film is actually based on the historic figure Countess Elizabeth Bathory, who has also been known as Countess Dracula from time to time. This is how the film derived its French title. In any event, Waldemar Daninsky is revived by a doctor who removes the silver bullets that originally destroyed him. Now restored to life, Waldemar and two young female students search for the tomb of Countess Wandesa de Nadasdy, a dreadful vampiress who maintained her youthful beauty by

consuming the blood of virgin girls. Naturally, they locate the vampire's tomb and she is revived by human blood. Countess Wandesa vampirizes one of the students, who then attacks her friend until Waldemar impales her with a stake. Now the Countess attacks the other young girl with plans of sacrificing her to Satan, resulting in a fierce battle between the vampire woman and the heroic Waldemar in his werewolf form.   The werewolf is destroyed when the young girl stabs him through the heart with a silver cross. Needless to say, the vampire countess is destroyed somewhere in all this mayhem. THE NIGHT OF THE WALPURGIS was released in the United States as THE WEREWOLF VS. THE VAMPIRE WOMAN during the mid 1970's.

JONATHAN

Iduna Film   1970

Controversial but prestigious is this color film made in West Germany. JONATHAN is a direct adaptation of Bram Stoker's Dracula in dialogue. However, the film is more of a political picture rather than one about vampirism in which the Dracula figure is compared to Germany's own real monster: Adolf Hitler.   The story depicts the relationship between the vampire and the town he dominates as a grim lesson in fascism.   The European town is under the rule of a mysterious cloaked figure who is also the head of a very powerful cult of vampires. The villagers decide that they have suffered long enough under the evil domination of the vampires and dispatch a heroic young man named Jonathan (Jurgen Jung), the film's Jonathan Harker, to the dreaded castle to destroy   them.   He eventually succeeds, driving the Dracula figure and his vampiric minions into the sea to drown.   Hans W. Geissendorfer's often slow but fascinating direction has been compared to that of F.W. Murnau and Roman Polanski's and the film has been praised by critics and film historians for its incredible allegorical style. The film was released in France as THE LAST COMBAT AGAINST THE

VAMPIRES.

COUNT DRACULA

Spanish 1970

In 1970, Spain announced an ambitious color production based on Bram Stoker's novel. The film was to be given an impressive budget, to be directed by Terence Fisher and to star horror star Vincent Price as Professor Van Helsing. Producer Harry Towers eventually cast Herbert Lom as Van Helsing and the film's direction was assigned to Jesus Franco. The role of Count Dracula went to Christopher Lee, who in the final production, portrays an older and mustached vampire as Bram Stoker had originally created in his novel. In fact, Lee, to that point in film history, was the first actor to portray the character correctly on the screen. The premise follows the Stoker novel relatively close, with Jonathan Harker arriving at Castle Dracula to be confronted by an older nobleman. With each intake of human blood, the vampire becomes younger in appearance. The film introduces the familiar characters of Van Helsing, Lucy and Mina, and concludes with a final showdown between Count Dracula and his arch enemy Van Helsing. Despite the low budget and the often tedious direction of Franco, the film does offer a serious and quite impressive enactment of the Stoker novel, with good to excellent performances by Lee and Lom.

COUNT YORGA-VAMPIRE

AIP 1970

Robert Quarry's performance as Count Yorga - vampire is perhaps one of the closest vampire characterizations to the image of Dracula. Quarry's vampire, like Christopher Lee's Count Dracula, is agile and very physical. Yorga is a polished gentleman on the surface while a devious and cunning bloodsucker within. One who will stop at nothing when attacking his victim to quench his desire for blood. Yorga was originally intended to be part of AIP's new image of horror figures during the early 1970's that also included Vincent Price's THE

ABOMINABLE DR. PHIBES (1970) and William Marshall's BLACULA (1972), to name only a couple. The film, directed by Bob Kelljan, is set among a modern Los Angeles, as Yorga and his vampire harem make the move onto a group of youngsters. The vampire meets his death when he receives a wooden broomstick through the heart. Amazingly, the film did very well at the box office, much better than Hammer's DRACULA A.D.- 1972 (1971) and THE SATANIC RITES OF DRACULA (1973), proving that a vampire could be as terrifying and interesting in the modern world as opposed to his traditional Gothic setting. The success of COUNT YORGA- VAMPIRE prompted AIP to immediately launched a sequel: THE RETURN OF COUNT YORGA (1971).

THE VAMPIRE LOVERS

Hammer 1970

1970 was unquestionably the year of the vampire film. It was also the year when Hammer executives decided to experiment with the vampire legend on film, thus screenwriters Tudor Gates and Michael Style wrote a screen adaptation of Sheridan Le Fanu's sensual vampire tale Carmilla. The film is slow moving but very vicious with nudity, lesbian sex, blood, violence, shock and suspense, all under the careful direction of Roy Ward Baker. Actress Ingrid Pitt portrays an erotic vampiress names Mircalla Karnstein. In the film, she literately sets her " bite" on the beautiful breasts of Madeline Smith. Peter Cushing also stars in the film as ruthless witch finder and vampire-killer General Von Spielsdorf, who protects his daughter Laura (played by Pippa Steele) from the clutches of Countess Karnstein by beheading the vampire in a chapel. Unfortunately, much of the sexual and graphic content of this film was cut by American sensors. THE VAMPIRE LOVERS is a fine tale of Gothic vampirism.

THE HOUSE THAT DRIPPED BLOOD

Amicus 1970

This marvelous anthology film from great Britain's Amicus International offers an interesting short segment pertaining to the vampire legend. The segment, entitled The Cloak, stars Paul Henderson as an aging horror film actor who is given a mysterious black cloak for his next film: CURSE OF THE BLOODSUCKERS. Whenever Henderson wears the cloak, he transforms into a fanged bloodsucker. While under the influence, he puts the bite on his leading lady Carla (Ingrid Pitt). We later learn that Carla is actually a vampire all along, who wanted him to become one of them in admiration of all his numerous vampire films. The comedy segment was directed by Peter Duffell and adapted from Robert Bloch's story of the same name.

SCARS OF DRACULA

Hammer 1970

Screenwriter John Elder gives Christopher Lee's Count Dracula new powers and supernatural capabilities. In order to entice Christopher Lee into another go around as Dracula, producers promised the actor that his character would be given generous dialogue and new characteristics in this his fifth Hammer - Dracula film. Unfortunately, this time around, the studio invested more into the character of Dracula and less into the sets. The result is a cheaper-looking production. In this film, Dracula is revived when a loyal vampire bat splatters blood over his remains. Once revived, the vampire takes out his revenge on unsuspecting travelers and on the inhabitants of a nearby village. The climax has the vampire king destroyed by a fiery bolt of lightning from the heavens above during a battle with the film's hero which is staged atop his castle. SCARS OF DRACULA was hammer's only attempt to recreate the style of the old Universal monster movies and is the studio's final period piece in the Dracula series.

HOUSE OF DARK SHADOWS

MGM 1970

Every fan of horror movies is familiar with the Dark Shadows television series that began in 1966 and continued up through 1971. The daytime soap opera gave life to America's most beloved vampire-Barnabas Collins (played by actor Jonathan Frid). In the TV soap Barnabas is released after one hundred and seventy-five years of imprisonment in a coffin by the lecherous Willie Loomis (played by John Karlen), and the rest, as they say, was history. The film HOUSE OF DARK SHADOWS actually sums up the vampire elements of the television soap, beginning with Barnabas's arrival at Collinswood Manor, where he immediately begins an unrelenting prey upon his wealthy and unsuspecting ancestors. The film moves very quickly, cramming six years of television history into ninety-seven minutes of film, but the excitement is grand, and the vampire elements are handled very well. The film goes straight for the throat, with good performances, strong atmosphere, impressive sets and an exciting new horror movie figure, Barnabas Collins. Barnabas was the new Dracula-like figure of the late 1960's and early 1970's, existing long before the sensation of FRIDAY THE 13TH's Jason and NIGHTMARE ON ELM STREET's Freddy Kruger. In short, he was the hottest new monster around. Frid is brilliant as the centuries-old vampire, and it is a shame that director Dan Curtis did not press upon MGM to produce a sequel in which Barnabas returns. Incidentally, Barnabas's destruction is quite clever. During the final moments of the film, the hero releases a wooden arrow through the vampire's heart before he can transform the heroine into one of the undead. The climatic sequence is one of the most powerful moment ever made for a vampire film. The film's sequel, NIGHT OF DARK SHADOWS (1972), dealt primarily with the witchcraft subplot of the television soap rather than the more exciting vampire elements. HOUSE OF DARK SHADOWS was, in 1970, an exciting and refreshing new vampire effort and was listed among one of the top ten films made that year. Today the film holds up rather well, especially if you are a diehard fan of Dark Shadows and Barnabas Collins. HOUSE OF DARK SHADOWS is available on video cassette and is recommended viewing.

THE LESBIAN VAMPIRES

Telecine & Fenix 1970

Another Spanish - German co-production directed by Jesus Franco. This film stars Dennis Price (SCARS OF DRACULA) and Susann Korda. The film is based on the novel Dracula's Guest by Bram Stoker and tells of a girl who dreams she is being seductively menaced by a lesbian vampire. The film is also known as THE STRANGE ADVENTURE OF JONATHAN HARKER and in Spain as THE SIGN OF THE VAMPIRE. Just as a note of reference, Universal's DRACULA'S DAUGHTER (1936) is also based on the same Bram Stoker novel and it is a much better film.

BLOOD SUCKERS

Titan International 1970

In this "clever and refreshingly original" film, vampirism is depicted as a sexual perversion and preference rather than a supernatural curse. Actor Patrick Mower is seduced into vampirism by a beautiful Greek woman (played by Imogen Hassal). Actors Peter Cushing, Edward Woodward and Patrick Macnee are wasted in this film which explores the theory that some men only achieve orgasm by the sucking of blood. The film was so bad that even the director removed his name from the final print.

GUESS WHAT HAPPENED TO COUNT DRACULA?

Merrick International 1970

A comedy spoof and color sex-ploitational film directed by Laurence Merrick that stars Des Robert as Count Dracula who, in the film, tries to adapt to contemporary ways of 1970 without loosing the traditional ways of Transylvania. Occasionally, Dracula sports around in his traditional black cape and tuxedo, but since the film takes place in modern day California, the vampire King also wears a turtleneck sweater and a double-breasted suit now and then. In America as Count Adrian, the vampire goes after the hippie-inhabited sunset strip and a beautiful young girl named Angelica (Claudia Barron). According to the legend established in this film, if Dracula sucks her blood three times, she will become a vampire. Surprisingly, Count Dracula wins, but before doing so, he must fight the film's hero (John Landon) and another supreme vampire named Imp (Frank Donato).

DRACULA VS. DR. FRANKENSTEIN

Fenix & Comtoir 1971

Another Jesus Franco Dracula epic co-produced by Spain and France. This time, Count Dracula (Howard Vernon) and Lady Dracula (Britt Nichols) return to their castle in the Carpathian mountains to initiate a new wave of vampirism. Combatting the vampires are Dr. Frankenstein (Dennis Price) and Morpho (Luis Barboo), his assistant, who create a monster which will destroy Dracula. There is also a Dr. Seward (Alberto Dalbes), who has hopes of finding a cure for the Count's vampiric condition. The low budget effort was released in France as DRACULA, PRISONER OF DOCTOR FRANKENSTEIN.

DRACULA A.D. - 1972

Hammer (1971)

I must say, this sixth film in the Hammer - Dracula series is the most disappointing of the lot. The film starts off very dramatically and promising, with Count Dracula (Christopher Lee) and Professor Van Helsing (Peter Cushing) engaged in a fierce battle on a runaway stagecoach bound to Castle Dracula. The coach never makes it to the castle and the battle is momentarily interrupted when the coach collides into a large tree. Both the vampire and the vampire-killer are tossed off the carriage. Suddenly, Dracula emerges from behind the coach impaled through the heart with a wooden spoke off of a wheel. The vampire desperately tries to remove the shaft from his own chest before Van Helsing regains consciousness, but it is too late. The Professor awakens in time to drive the spoke deeper, sending the vampire to the hereafter once more. The film then shifts from its Gothic setting to modern day London, England, and from this point, the film takes on a new mood not worthy of its Gothic predecessors. Somehow Chris Lee's Dracula just does not work very well in modern day London. The screenplay written by Don Houghton keeps the vampire within the ruins of a desecrated church throughout the remaining film. His resurrection is similar to that in TASTE THE BLOOD OF DRACULA. This time, actor Christopher Neame is the descendant of an evil disciple who revives the vampire after a century and a half of sleep. Peter Cushing also plays a descendant of the original Van Helsing who originally destroyed the vampire during the more dramatic opening sequence of this film. Thus Dracula is out for revenge on his nemesis' descendants. It is amazing that a low budget film like COUNT YORGA-VAMPIRE did much better at the box office than this film. Hammer's attempt to bump the character of Dracula to modern day to appeal to a more youthful audience just did not work very well, but Warner Brothers, the film's American distributor and financier, put the pressure on Hammer to come up with a Dracula film set in modern times in hopes of capturing the success of films like COUNT YORGA-VAMPIRE (1970) and HOUSE OF DARK SHADOWS (1970). Unfortunately, the idea just did not work. Funny thing; it's amazing how most Gothic vampire films usually hold up much better than vampires set in modern times. There are a few exceptions to the rule, that is, regarding films of the late 1960's and early 1970's.

BLOODTHIRSTY EYES
Toho   1971

Released in America as THE LAKE OF DRACULA, this film, directed by Michio Yamamoto, despite its Oriental origin,

is mostly a modern Gothic horror film with extremely satisfying photography. In many ways, the film imitates the style established in the Hammer Dracula films, depicting the vampire as a dynamic figure. The film opens with a little girl chasing her dog through a cave. She passes a lake under a red sky and comes upon a castle hidden in the woods. There she encounters an old man, a pale young girl and a mysterious young gentleman with golden eyes. The film resumes years later with the girl as an adult. She now considers the entire experience to be nothing more than a childhood nightmare, but this is not so. A pale-faced Oriental vampire arrives in her town and places several mortals under his spell, including the woman's sister. Soon her sister dies and re-awakens in the morgue, as well as other victims caught in the vampire's spell. We then discover through the film's hero that the vampire is actually the descendant of Count Dracula himself, who impregnated an Oriental woman. The boy had been born with golden eyes and a savage bloodthirsty nature. The fiendish vampire is eventually destroyed in a scene inspired by Hammer's DRACULA HAS RISEN FROM THE GRAVE (1968). The vampire inadvertently trips, plunging backwards over a banister and falling onto a wooden stake that plunges through his heart. BLOODTHIRSTY EYES is one of those rare vampire films that actually work in a modern setting.

THE RETURN OF COUNT YORGA
AIP   1971

COUNT YORGA - VAMPIRE proved to be very successful at the box office, but not much could be said for this sequel in terms of box office appeal. Directed again by Kelljan, THE RETURN OF COUNT YORGA features actor Robert Quarry as Count Yorga, who suddenly and miraculously appears at a masquerade party after having been destroyed during the climax of the first film. His revival is never explained. Once again Yorga

spreads terror among the youth of California with the aide of his harem of vampires. The master vampire is eventually destroyed, this time with a silver-tipped dagger. The low production values seem to take its toll on the film's appearance, but Quarry still manages to give a credible performance as the vampire Yorga.

LUST FOR A VAMPIRE
Hammer   1971

Originally, this film was intended to star Peter Cushing under Terence Fisher's direction. However, Cushing bowed out to star in another film and Fisher was unavailable. Thus Jimmy Sangster took on the film's direction. As a result of Sangster's weak direction, the film is a below average Hammer vampire vehicle and an inconsistent sequel to Hammer's THE VAMPIRE LOVERS (1970). The film has no relation to the Sheridan Le Fanu novel and was produced with only box office returns in mind, as evident by Hammer's lack of interest in terms of budget, casting and use of cheap thrills that have become cliche to the most sordid of vampire films. Replacing Ingrid Pitt as Mircalla is Yutte Stensgaard, who is unconvincing as the vampire figure. Actor Ralph Bates in equally poor in the role originally intended for Cushing. The weak premise, written by Tudor Gates, has Mircalla revived by Count Karnstein (played by Mike Raven). She is enrolled into an all girl's school near the castle where she seduces her classmates with lesbian sex and then turns them into "chop liver!" During the film's climax, Mircalla is impaled by a burning rafter and sentenced to eternal death forever. LUST FOR A VAMPIRE was Hammer's attempt to put the sex back into the genre, and using the word LUST in the title was a good start. The film uses generous amounts of blood and unnecessary violence to achieve it's mood and does not hold up nearly as well as the original film. Finally, Bates, who is usually a good actor, is unfortunately wasted here.

COUNTESS DRACULA

Hammer   1971

The cinema's most famous film concerning the legend of Countess Elizabeth Bathory. As legend has it, Bathory use to bathe in the blood of young virgin girls to restore her youthful appearance; thus the name Countess Dracula. In the film, the deranged Countess is portrayed by Ingrid Pitt. Although the direction of Peter Sasdy is tedious and slow moving at times, the film is an excellent, dramatic piece, void of Hammer's usual dramatics and violence.

BLACULA

AIP   1971

American International Pictures (AIP) was on a roll, and their next vampire entry was perhaps its most original and refreshing despite its commercial title. BLACULA is a surprisingly good low budget effort from producer Joseph T. Naar. The film intelligently succeeds in combining the familiar Dracula legend with the creation of a new vampire terror. The subplot about slavery issues was added to Andy Brown's script by actor William Marshall, who, in the film, plays Prince Mamuwalde; better known as Blacula! In 1815, the Prince and his wife Luva (Vonette McGee) journey to Castle Dracula to influence the Count to place an embargo on the slave trade. Their plans are thwarted when the bigoted Count Dracula (magnificently played by Charles Macaulay) places a curse on the Prince and seals him in a coffin for one hundred and fifty years. As history has it, Dracula is eventually destroyed for being the ruthless and savage vampire that he is, but the Prince lives on, sealed in Dracula's coffin for a century and a half, until one day, two gay interior decorators unseal the coffin and release one of cinema's most brutal vampires onto modern society. The Negro vampire plagues the city of modern day Los Angeles until he happens across a beautiful reincarnation of his long-dead Princess Luva. Blacula looses his refound

Princess at the mercy of vampire hunters, destroying his only reason to live. Blacula courageously and voluntarily exposes himself to the sun's lethal rays and reduces to dust forever. BLACULA is quite impressive and should not be missed by fans of vampire films.

VAMPIRE   CIRCUS

Hammer   1971

One of Hammer's more exciting and original vampire efforts from the 1970's. The film features a new vampire, Count Mitterhouse (Robert Tayman), who has fangs the size of a King Cobra! The vampire terrorizes the Serbian countryside, draining the blood of innocent children. The villagers eventually storm the vampire's castle and drive a wooden stake through the savage beast's heart. But several months later, strange things begin to occur when Mitterhouse's cousin, Emil (played by Anthony Corlan) arrives into town. Emil leads a circus of freaks and oddities and it is he who revives his vampiric cousin to plague the countryside once more. VAMPIRE CIRCUS is definitely Hammer's goriest vampire film. The premise is a bit unusual, bit it works very well and still manages to hold up rather well by today's standards. Director Robert Young filmed many sensual and violent scenes that were edited by American censors, which is unfortunate. Fans of Hammer films will not want to miss this one!

VAMPIRE MEN OF THE LOST PLANET

Independent   Intl.   1971

John Carradine strikes again with another "Academy Award-winning" performance in this low budget Al Adamson-produced and directed vehicle. A scientist (Carradine) traces an epidemic of vampire attacks on Earth to a strange planet with the aide of stock footage from other low budget films. We eventually discover that vampirism, as we know it, originated in outer space. Boy, I'm sure the guys at Hammer really appreciated this picture! John Carradine leads an expedition

into space to investigate the source of vampirism. Is it possible that writer Susan McNair saw PLANET OF THE VAMPIRES before writing this film? In any event, the plot crams eighty-five minutes of neck bites, spear stabbings, cannibalism and crawfish monsters with cheap sets, poor photography and horrendous performances. This bomb of a film is also known as HORROR OF THE BLOOD MONSTERS.

THE VELVET VAMPIRE

New World   1971

It seems that most of the vampire films in which the central vampire is a female involves lesbianism. For example, the vampiress of this film (played by Celeste Yarnell) has no quarrels with drinking male blood, however, she usually prefers women as her sex partner. This tradition can be traced as far back as Sheridan Le Fanu's novel Carmilla and the vintage horror films VAMPYR (1931) and DRACULA'S DAUGHTER (1936). THE VELVET VAMPIRE falls within this category. Directed by Stephanie Rothman, the erotic film features actress Celeste Yarnell as a very striking Diane LeFanu (a name giving homage to writer Sheridan LeFanu), a relative of the Karnsteins who invites a young married couple stranded in the desert into her home. Little do they know that their hostess is a vampire with plans of seducing and then killing each of them. The bisexual elements are soft-core and the transfer of the vampire legend is handled stylishly by the film's director. The film was re-released under the simply ludicrous title, CEMETERY GIRLS.

DAUGHTERS OF DARKNESS

Gemini   1971

Made in Belgium by director Harry Kumel, DAUGHTERS OF DARKNESS is based on the novel Countess Dracula by Michael Parry. The film tells how Countess Elizabeth Bathory (Delphine Seyrig) survives into the 1970's as an undead vampire. The modernized Countess and her companion Ilona (Andrea Rau) check into an almost deserted European hotel where a sadist (played by John " Dark Shadows" Karlen) kills Ilona. In revenge, the Countess puts the bite on Karlen's wife, who now becomes a vampire herself, joining forces with Bathory. In the film's most disturbing sequence, Countess Bathory and her new mistress slash Karlen's wrist and literally consume all of his blood. The vampire's death in this film comes about accidentally. DAUGHTERS OF DARKNESS was one of the few films to depict the legendary Countess Elizabeth Bathory as a real vampire, unlike the Hammer film COUNTESS DRACULA of the same year which simply leaves any hints of vampirism to the minds of its viewers, depicting the Countess as a demented lunatic.

CAPTAIN KRONOS: VAMPIRE HUNTER

Hammer   1972

Imagine a nineteenth century swashbuckler who specializes in slaying vampires! In this color film written and directed by Brian Clemens, Captain Kronos (Horst Janson) is a swashbuckler who battles a vampire lord in a sword fight. Naturally, Kronos defeats the vampire by impaling him with a sword through the heart. Together, the vampire and his mistress (Wanda Ventham) age into withered corpses after being slain. The swashbuckling theme was Hammer's attempt to pump originality and vibrance into their vampire films. CAPTAIN KRONOS: VAMPIRE HUNTER is actually an entertaining film, but the film failed miserably at the box office. A sequel was announced by Hammer, but the film never made it past the post-production stages. Today we have BUFFY- THE VAMPIRE SLAYER (1992), which is nothing more than a glorified post- Ninja Turtles version of this Hammer film.

THE DEATHMASTER

RF Productions   1972

Originally announced as KHORDA, this film stars actor Robert Quarry (of COUNT YORGA fame) as a fully-fanged, long-haired hippie vampire who is washed onto the California coast to become a guru for many young hippies. The low budget feature was Quarry's last vampire film and was not nearly as successful as his previous COUNT YORGA films. Sounds like an early version of THE LOST BOYS (1987) with Quarry as an older Kiefer Sutherland. Well, maybe not!

THE GREAT LOVE OF COUNT DRACULA

Janus Productions   1972

Actor Paul Naschy stars in this Spanish-made vampire film as Count Dracula himself. Count Dracula makes a fatal mistake by falling in love with a mortal woman (his great love). The Count actually becomes emotionally involved and rather than endangering her life with his unquenchable desire for human blood, the vampire drives a wooden stake through his heart. Naschy's portrayal of a sympathetic vampire and a victim of his own curse which forces him to kill, is a fascinating variation on the Dracula theme. Dracula dies a hero and not a villain in this film, making movie history. THE GREAT LOVE OF COUNT DRACULA is directed by Javier Aguirre.

TWINS OF EVIL

Hammer   1972

Writer Tudor Gates, in his third and final installment to Hammer's Carmilla series, effectively combines the Sheridan Le Fanu tale with tales of witch hunting and burning at the stake. In this film, Mircalla (now played by Katya Keith) is inadvertently revived by the newest of the Karnstein descendants, Count Karnstein (Damien Thomas) in his attempt to summon Satan. Identical twins Maria and Frieda Gelhourn (Madeline and Mary Collinson) are the first to fall prey to the vampire, but their uncle (played by Peter Cushing) arrives on the scene in time to decapitate Mircalla and to drive a wooden stake her through her heart. TWINS OF EVIL is directed by John Hough with effectively strong atmosphere, good sets and some good camera work by Stan Samworth. It is evident that Hammer executives invested more into this production than in its predecessors. Cushing is exceptionally great as Gustav Weil, the head of a witch hunting group called the Brotherhood and Damien Thomas is convincing as a demon worshiper and vampire.

GRAVE OF THE VAMPIRE

Independent   1972

Grim and unusual vampire tale in which a woman is raped by Count Dracula and later has a baby who drinks his mother's blood out of a bottle. Michael Pataki plays the adult vampire. The film is also known as SEED OF TERROR.

THE DAUGHTER OF DRACULA

Comptoir   1972

Director Jesus Franco strikes again in this Spanish, French, Portuguese co-production. DAUGHTERS OF DARKNESS is another variation on the Carmilla legend in which actress Britt Nichols portrays the modern-day vampiress while actor Howard Vernon plays Count Karnstein. The film offers good atmospheric photography and is actually less tedious than TERROR IN THE CRYPT (1970).

VOODOO   HEARTBEAT

Compass   1972

Horrible, horrible film in which a man periodically transforms into a crazed bloodsucker. The pseudo-vampire runs around with two silly-looking elongated fangs protruding from his mouth is broad daylight.

THE SCREAMING DEAD

Fenix   1972

Jesus Franco must be Spain's leading horror film-maker. The man has simply made more horror films than Terence Fisher and George Romero put together. It's a shame the quality of most of his films are not equivalent to Fisher's. In any event, THE SCREAMING DEAD is another Spanish-made Dracula epic in which Dr. Seward drives a silver spike into Dracula's heart. The fiend turns into a large bat and dies. Now Dr.

Frankenstein revives the vampire by splattering the blood of an innocent girl on his ashes. Frankenstein has plans of enslaving the vampire. Now Howard Vernon as a green-faced Count Dracula begins draining the blood of locals until a revengeful gypsy woman sends a werewolf to kill the fiend. As guessed, the film ends in a nasty free-for-all battle, Franco-style. Vernon also played Count Karnstein in Franco's THE DAUGHTER OF DRACULA (1972).

DRACULA: THE BLOODLINE CONTINUES

Profilmes   1972

Another bizarre variation on Stoker's Dracula figure. In this Spanish-made film, an aging Count Dracula (played by Narciso Ibanez Menta) hopes to insure a suitably vigorous heir to his ghoulish dynasty, so he invites his pregnant niece to the castle and exchanges her evening wine with fresh blood to give the unborn a taste of life among the undead. It is later revealed that the Dracula family has stooped to incest to keep the bloodline alive. Therefore, her baby is the new hope for the family. Totally repulsed, the woman (Tina Saenz) kills her own child and stakes the entire family. In a struggle with one of Dracula's servants, she inadvertently trips over her supposedly dead child. The child begins sucking on her blood! So much for killing the family bloodline. Although the Lazarus Kaplan script sets the film in contemporary time, DRACULA: THE BLOODLINE CONTINUES offers pleasing Gothic atmosphere, stylish dream sequences, and an abundance of sex, nudity and gore. The film is directed by Leon Klimovsky and is also known as THE SAGA OF THE DRACULAS.

SCREAM BLACULA, SCREAM

AIP   1972

Not much could be said for this sequel to the very successful film BLACULA. The sequel is directed by Bob Kelljan as a combination of vampirism and voodooism. The film tells how a high priest (Richard Lawson) performs a voodoo ritual that inadvertently revives Prince Mamuwalde. The vampire is eventually destroyed when a wooden stake is driven through a voodoo doll replica of himself. The film was not nearly as successful as the original film, therefore any attempt to make a sequel was halted. Actor William Marshall once described the film's failure as a result of its weak and confusing script.

THE BODY BENEATH

Nova International   1972

Inadequate production values are the root of this film's failure at the box office. Directed by Andy Milligan THE BODY BENEATH stars actor Gavin Reed as a vampire who comes to London to prey upon a British family. The vampire eventually comes across Dracula's Carfax Abbey.

DRACULA VS. FRANKENSTEIN

Independent   1972

Originally planned for production under the title BLOOD OF FRANKENSTEIN, this mundane low budget horror film eventually resulted in the inevitable and inadvertent confrontation between the screen's most infamous monsters: Count Dracula and the Frankenstein Monster. I say resulted because the film underwent numerous changes during production, and neither the cast nor the filmmakers had no idea where this film was heading or that there would be such a confrontation. Apparently the original plot was simply going nowhere, and producer Al Adamson came up with the idea of staging a confrontation between the two monsters to actually beef up interest in this otherwise dull film. I remember viewing this movie for the first time as a pre-teenager at the local drive-in. I would have never thought that the film would have resulted in such a dramatic confrontation when I viewed the film for the first time. For me, the confrontation set in a wooded area is still fresh in my memory. The scene in which Dracula (played by Zandor Vorkov) battles the hideous Frankenstein Monster (played by John Bloom) is effectively staged by director Al Adamson and is the film's highlight and only credible moment. The plot is totally ludicrous, and the performances are horrendous. Count Dracula wishes to revive the dormant Frankenstein Monster. To do this, he takes the monster's body to an amusement park's demented operator, Dr. Durea (played by J. Carrol Naish), who is really Dr. Frankenstein. The scientist devises a serum from the blood of young girls axed and beheaded by his servants Groton and Grabo (played by Lon Chaney, Jr. and Angelo Rossito). The serum enables the doctor to revive the monster to its full force. Dracula also hopes that the serum will enable him to endure sunlight. Total mayhem follows as Dr. Frankenstein is beheaded in his own Chamber of Horrors, while Groton his shot to death by the police. Meanwhile, Dracula uses the Frankenstein Monster to abduct his love interest (played by Regina Carrol) to a nearby chapel where his coffin is hidden. There, the vampire begins a ritual that will make her a creature of the night like himself, but when the monster sees the helpless young girl about to perish at the touch of the vampire's fangs, the Frankenstein Monster attacks Dracula, and a fierce battle between the two monsters ensues. Dracula literally rips the Frankenstein Monster to pieces, but the sun reduces him to a rotted corpse before he can reach the safety of his coffin. The final scene in which Dracula races to his coffin before the sun rises is one of the most dramatic moments in vampire cinema. It is a shame, however, to see actors Lon Chaney, Jr. and J. Carroll Naish reduced to such pitiful roles. This amateurish production is not half bad when given a chance and viewed from start to finish.

THE NIGHT STALKER

Curtis Productions 1972

Writer, producer and director Dan Curtis made television history for bringing to life the famous vampire Barnabas Collins from Dark Shadows. He also made history with his television series The Night Stalker, which he adapted into a made for television film in 1972. The film made history when over seventy-five million viewers tuned in the night this film premiered on television. Screenwriter Richard Matheson adapted the story by John Rice, while John Llewellyn Moxey directed. Actor Darren McGavin plays investigative reporter Carl Kolchak, who follows a series of vampire related murders in Las Vegas. The police do not believe Kolchak's theory of vampirism, so he sets off on his own to locate the vampire's lair. Actor Barry Atwater plays the very menacing and cunning vampire Janos Skorzeny. In the film, Kolchak does manage to drive a wooden stake through the beast's heart but not until some very hair-raising moments.

THE SATANIC RITES OF DRACULA

Hammer 1973

Hammer began production on this film before the box-office results were in from the commercial failure DRACULA A.D. -1972 (1971). The studio was stuck with another Dracula outing set in modern-day London, and Warner Brothers decided not to release the film in America as agreed upon, at least not until 1979, when the American studio issued the film under the ridiculous title DRACULA AND HIS VAMPIRE BRIDES. The poor American marketing of this film is unfortunate because THE SATANIC RITES OF DRACULA is actually a much better film than DRACULA A.D. - 1972, offering a much more interesting and original premise. To enjoy the film, one must accept it for what it really is and not compare it to its Gothic predecessors. The Don Houghton screenplay depicts Count Dracula (Christopher Lee) as a larger than life Howard Hughes-like figurehead obsessed with destroying the world by some form of black plague via a virus that only he possesses. Peter Cushing returns to the role of Professor Van Helsing, who leads a crusade against the evil vampire until he is able to drive a wooden stake through his heart, again. Director Alan

Gibson proves that he cannot handle the simplest of materials and the film marked the downfall and end of the long Hammer-Dracula series that began in 1958 with HORROR OF DRACULA. In retrospect, THE SATANIC RITES OF DRACULA would not have received such a bad reception at theaters had DRACULA A.D. - 1972 not given fans such a bad taste.

THE LEGEND OF THE SEVEN GOLDEN VAMPIRES

Hammer 1973-1974

Immediately after the release of THE SATANIC RITES OF DRACULA, Hammer began production on another Dracula film intended to star Christopher Lee and Peter Cushing. However, Lee was not very pleased with the direction his immortal character was heading towards, thus he decided to bow out, which is a shame because this film manages to maintain a Gothic atmosphere. Hammer proceeded with production despite Lee's decision, replacing the actor with John Forbes Robertson as Dracula. The film was a co-production between Hammer and the Shaw Brothers of Hong Kong, since Warner would no longer be involved in the Dracula series after the poor box office returns generated from DRACULA A.D.-1972. One of the stipulations in the agreement between Hammer and the Shaw Brothers was that there be some kind of martial arts footage and subplot. The result is a cross between the Gothic Dracula legend and Kung Fu! The film takes place in the Orient where the legendary Seven Golden Vampires ride across the screen mounted on their demonic horses and armed with swords, evil spirits and an army of mindless zombies; all of which are commanded by one person, Count Dracula! Professor Van Helsing ventures to the Far East to investigate rumors of Satanic worshipping and confronts his life-long nemesis, and they once again engage in battle, this time larger than life. THE LEGEND OF THE SEVEN GOLDEN VAMPIRES is directed by Roy Ward Baker with heavy

Gothic atmosphere and the mysticism of the Orient. Had Hammer invested more into this film, the outcome could have actually been brilliant.

DRACULA

Curtis productions 1973

Academy-Award winning actor Jack Palance is superb as a very sympathetic Count Dracula in this Dan Curtis production also made for television. The film, loosely based on Bram Stoker's novel by screenwriter Richard Matheson, tells of Jonathan Harker's journey to Castle Dracula and Dracula's journey to England to claim the reincarnation of a woman he once loved hundreds of years ago. The script cleverly combines the true legend of Vlad Tepes (the real life warrior who Count Dracula was originally based upon) and the Stoker novel. Matheson has eliminated many of the familiar characters featured in the Stoker novel and has incorporated new characters, new situations and clever plot twists. In this version, Dracula is destroyed by the sun's rays in a dramatic confrontation between the vampire and Professor Van Helsing (played brilliantly by Nigel Davenport). DRACULA received very good ratings when aired on television and is perhaps one of producer Dan Curtis's better quality television films.

THE DEVIL'S WEDDING NIGHT

AIP 1973

Originally planned under the title COUNTESS DRACULA, this film is a bizarre combination of the Dracula legend and the legend of Elizabeth Bathory. In the film actor Mark Damon portrays twin brothers Fritz and Karl. Karl traces an ancient ring to Castle Karnstein in Transylvania. His journey eventually leads him to Castle Dracula, where he becomes possessed by the spirit of Dracula himself. Meanwhile Fritz journeys to Castle Dracula in search of his brother and instead he finds a Countess (Bathory?) with fangs and is forced to engage in a battle with her thugs. Eventually, the Countess is destroyed, and Fritz drives a wooden stake through Karl's heart. This confusing film was directed by Roger Corman.

SON OF DRACULA
Apple Films 1973

Ringo Starr of Beetles fame plays Count Down, son of Count Dracula, who is portrayed by singer Harry Nilsson. Count Down is a musician who plays with a rock band in the basement of Castle Dracula. The plot involves the offspring's discontent with replacing his father as an Overlord Of The Netherworld along with such famous monsters as the Wolfman, the Mummy, the Frankenstein Monster and others. The film was directed in tongue-in-cheek style by Freddie Francis, who also directed the horror films THE EVIL OF FRANKENSTEIN (1964), DRACULA HAS RISEN FROM THE GRAVE (1968), and THE LEGEND OF THE WEREWOLF (1974).

BLOOD FOR DRACULA
Warhol 1973

Directed by Paul Morissey for the late Andy Warhol's underground film company, BLOOD FOR DRACULA stars actor Udo Keir as Count Dracula. The film introduces the concept that Dracula can only stomach the blood of virgins. The film is very graphic and gory, especially the climax in which Dracula's arms and legs are hacked off by the film's hero. As guessed, blood gushes everywhere. BLOOD FOR DRACULA is also known as ANDY WARHOL'S DRACULA. The film is also available on video under its original X-rated, uncut version.

EROTIKILL
Eurocine 1973

Jesus Franco actually stars in this unusual vampire film that he also produced and directed (under the fictitious name of J.P. Johnson). In the film he plays an investigative reporter tracing a string of vampire-like killings (He's no Carl Kolchak!). Franco's wife, who is the film's leading actress Lina Romay, plays the lead vampire as a sex goddess. She kills off the film's characters in a combination of traditional throat-ripping and erotic deep-throating. The film is poorly dubbed in English and offers Franco's usual style of meaningless graphic violence. EROTIKILL is also known as THE BARE BREASTED COUNTESS.

VAMPIRA
1973

A comedy produced by Jack Wiener starring the late actor David Niven as an ultra-suave Count Dracula, complete with fangs, mustache and widow's peak. Vampira (Teresa Graves), Dracula's countess, becomes upset when she learns that the dirty old man is involved with lovely young women. Niven makes an interesting Dracula, but the comedy trappings are no different than DRACULA - THE DIRTY OLD MAN (1970). Also known as OLD DRACULA.

THE BLOOD SPLATTERED BRIDE
Independent 1974

Another film based on the sensual occult tale Carmilla by Sheridan Le Fanu. The film features graphic scenes of bloody violence and erotic lesbian romance. A poor, low budget adaptation of the novel, especially when there are so many more quality film versions of Carmilla available to the enthusiast. THE BLOOD SPLATTERED BRIDE is ideal for the fan of obscure splatter and exploitation films.

NIGHT OF THE SORCERERS
Independent 1974

A macabre tale of murder, violence, rape and unquenchable lusts set deep in the jungles of the Congo, where beautiful young women are sacrificed to the vampire leopard women. The vampire species are very savage and lethal in this film. Unfortunately, the film itself is twice as lethal. Poor script, horrible acting and, of course, minuscule budget are all the reasons why this film is horrible, destroying the all too few moments of good horror. NIGHT OF THE SORCERERS is not one of the better early 1970's vampire films.

BLOOD
Independent 1974

Director Andy Milligan's grotty, neo-porno vampire epic in which the Wolf Man's son and Dracula's daughter decide to settle down somewhere in Staten Island. Poor excuse for a vampire film. Next to H.G. Lewis, Milligan is regarded as the leading filmmaker of splatter movies. This should give you an indication of the nature of this film. BLOOD was Milligan's final film.

TENDER DRACULA OR THE CONFESSIONS OF A BLOODSUCKER
AIP 1974

Actor Peter Cushing traveled to France to star as Count Dracula himself in this light-hearted comedy-horror film. It is ironic that Cushing portrays a vampire here since most of his film career was devoted to playing the famous vampire killer Van Helsing in many of the Hammer-Dracula films. In this film directed by Alain Robbe-Grillet, Cushing portrays an aging horror actor who wants so much to desert the genre for a more versatile career. Ironically, the storyline resembles the actor's career in horror films. The film was never issued in America, at least not to this writer's knowledge.

DRACULA'S DOG
Crown International 1975

Count Dracula finally goes to the dogs? Just when you thought that Hollywood had made the shabbiest Dracula epic, Crown International comes along and releases this low budget fiasco from director Albert Band. The film stars Michael Pataki as Count Dracula, and together with his hell-spawned canine, the vampire wreaks terror in modern Los Angeles as he tries to locate his only living relative. Actors Reggie Nalder and Jose Ferrer have supporting roles.

LEMORA- LADY DRACULA

Blackburn   1975

Also known as LEMORA - A CHILD'S TALE OF THE SUPERNATURAL, this film features actress Cheryl Smith as Lila Lee, a young girl who leaves her repressive church in search of her long-lost gangster father. In her travel, Lila encounters Lemora (Lesley Gilb), an elegant, sexy vampire who seduces her with drink, dancing, raw meat and sex- vampire style. The low budget film is written and directed by Richard Blackburn, who later co-wrote EATING RAOUL. Blackburn tries to establish an artistic mood, using the vampire as a mode of female liberation. The film has many flaws. For example, it is often hard to follow Blackburn's confusing script and the film suffers from severe economic problems. The same film today with a multi-million dollar budget under the proper direction of say, Ridley Scott or Tim Burton, would produce an entertaining horror fantasy. What a little money can do? In any event, LEMORA- LADY DRACULA is regarded as a cult classic.

MARY MARY, BLOODY MARY

Summit   1975

Former model and ex-Mrs. DeLorean Christina Ferrare is featured in this film as a sexy lesbian vampire- artist named Mary, of course, whose victims are dying to quench her thirst for blood. Soon Mary's insatiable desire for blood threatens those she loves and cares about. John Carradine plays her father, who, together with the Mexican authorities, tries to come between her and her next victim's throat. Mary eventually kills her lesbian lover in a bloody bathtub scene and she is accused of committing other bloody murders around town. We soon discover that Carradine is actually the vampire responsible for most of the murders. Talk about plot twists? The film is played very straight, and actress Ferrare almost kills the film, but thanks to some slick direction by Juan Lopez Moctezuma and a good supporting cast, the film rises above her weak performance. Much better, if you can

believe, and in the same mode as the made for television film I DESIRE (1982).

MARTIN

Braddock Associates   1975

Writer - director George A. Romero is the true talent behind the film MARTIN. The film deals with the mentally ill, primarily Martin (played by John Amplas), who is believed to have inherited the family curse: vampirism. The teenage boy, who believes himself to be eighty-four years old, attacks women in their sleep by drugging them first and then slitting their arms and drinking their blood. The witty script has Martin believing that he is actually a vampire, but we, the viewers, know that he is suffering from his feelings of sexual inadequacy and severe repressiveness of his emotions. The clever hallucinations in which Martin envisages his vampiric behavior as some kind of evil romanticism is inserted into the film in black and white in this otherwise color film. Unlike Romero's other films (DAWN OF THE DEAD -1978; CREEPSHOW- 1982; DAY OF THE DEAD - 1985), MARTIN does not overflow with an abundance of blood and gore, even when Martin is wrongly staked through the heart by his cousin. The film is the most thorough re-examination of the vampire figure to this date.

RABID

Cinepix   1976

David Cronenberg's film RABID is a particularly interesting departure to the vampire theme. In this film, a woman (played by ex-porno star Marilyn Chambers) becomes the victim of a new technique in plastic surgery. A side effect creates a retractable syringe-like growth in her arm pit. Soon she feels compelled to attack people with her syringe for human blood in order to stay alive. Her victims develop a rabies-like disease which causes a form of homicidal mania. RABID moves at a very fast pace and is often predictable, but depicts its story in a more elaborate fashion than

Cronenberg's earlier film SHIVERS (1976).

BLOOD RELATIONS

Netherland Films   1977

A very unusual and restrained vampire film in which a young nurse discovers that Dr. Steiger (Maxim Hamel) is stealing blood plasma because he is a vampire. Steiger belongs to a cult of vampires who also require the same type of feeding patterns. Claiming to be a vampire too, she infiltrates the cult, but her plans ultimately fail. The film is directed by Wim Linder in a fashion similar to Roman Polanski's ROSEMARY'S BABY (1968).

DEAD OF NIGHT

Curtis Productions   1977

Not to be confused with the 1945 British Ghost film, DEAD OF NIGHT is a made for television anthology film from producer- director Dan (DARK SHADOWS & THE NIGHT STALKER) Curtis in which one of the segments include a tale about a vampire's lair in a small village. Ed Begley, Jr. and Patrick Macnee star in this quickly made, undoubtedly forgotten film.

DRACULA: FATHER AND SON

Concorde   1977

Actor Christopher Lee is considered to be one of the great movie Draculas, and I might add, with some very good films to his credit. Film's such as Hammer's HORROR OF DRACULA (1958), DRACULA-PRINCE OF DARKNESS (1964) and DRACULA HAS RISEN FROM THE GRAVE (1968). In fact, no other actor has portrayed the King of Vampires more than Lee. Eight times to be exact. In this spoof on the Dracula legend, Lee plays the title role for laughs. Old Dracula wants his son to take over as Lord of the Vampires. The trouble is, young Dracula would rather be a florist before becoming some supreme monster. The film mixes blood with laughs, and it is good to see Lee as Dracula after a four year absence from the role. The actor has yet to play the vampire King since the release of this 1977 film.

DRACULA

Universal 1979

John Badham's DRACULA has received so much criticism since its release in 1979 alongside NOSFERATU (1979) and LOVE AT FIRST BITE (1979). Werner Herzog's NOSFERATU is a tale of pure horror while Stan Dragoti's LOVE AT FIRST BITE is a camp parody on the Dracula legend. Both Herzog and Dragoti's films work well as the films that they are intended to be. However, I must agree with film historians and critics that Badham's DRACULA steers an uneasy course between the two films, weather intentional or unintentional. I do feel the film is genuine in its attempt to be that of horror, however glorified and flashy the cast appears. The film takes its characters serious, especially Dracula. Dracula is portrayed by handsome Frank Langella as a suave Valentino-like hero with burning, hypnotic eyes, who sweeps actress Kate Nelligan off her feet with all the decadence his character can possibly possess. True, Langella's Dracula does not match the mysteriousness that Bela Lugosi's Count Dracula permeates, nor does he offer the combination of suaveness and menace that Christopher Lee's Dracula possesses. Nevertheless, Langella's Dracula is frightfully precise as an incarnation of pure evil, packaged and delivered in pretty wrapping. Langella's Dracula is quite the opposite of Klaus Kinski's characterization in NOSFERATU (1979). In DRACULA there are moments of great horror as when the Count scales down the side of a wall head first (taken directly from Bram Stoker's novel and overlooked by both Universal's 1931 version and Hammer's 1958 version). There is also a scene in which Professor Van Helsing (played by legendary actor Lord Laurence Olivier) confronts his vampiric daughter Lucy. The foul creature of the night attacks her father as she chants to him in Dutch; her eyes ablaze in fiery red. The film also offers other thrilling moments such as when a white horse smells out the grave site of Van Helsing's recently buried and vampirized daughter. The horse proceeds to dig up the grave with its hoofs. This effective sequence was a clever addition the vampire folklore. Badham's DRACULA, in my opinion, is first rate, and Langella's Dracula is quite fascinating in a seductive way. Kate Nelligen is brilliant as Lucy Harker and Laurence Olivier's Van Helsing is reminiscent of Peter Seller's Inspector Closeau without the comedy antics. However, Langella is by far the high point of the film. True, the film is a bit too modern to be called Victorian, and Badham unfortunately wastes the magnificent sets, but the good aspects certainly outweigh the bad. The special effects are great and the sweeping music score by John Williams is near brilliant. DRACULA, in my opinion, is a brilliant film. Yes, I agree, the film lacks fangs and blood and I think the lack of these accessaries disappointed diehard fans. Perhaps Francis Coppala's soon to be released version will strike a happy medium.

SALEM'S LOT

Warner 1979

Tobe Hooper's SALEM'S LOT is based on Stephen King's novel Jerusalem's Lot, and because the film was made for television, it does not present too many disturbing and scary moments to avoid making a television taboo. The film takes its central vampire figure very serious, keeping the monster unseen through three quarters of the film, which is actually a blessing in disguise because the Paul Monash script misleadingly elevates the viewer's expectations of Barlow, the ringleader and procurer of the vampire village (by three quarters of the film, most of the town of Jerusalem's Lot is unconvincingly transformed into undead creatures by the unseen vampire leader). Barlow is depicted as a cunning centuries-old creature. The viewer is let down when Barlow makes his first meaningless appearance as he crashes through a kitchen window to attack a family and local priest. It would appear that this meaningless scene was just thrown in to spice things up in this otherwise lengthy and boring flick. Here is a vampire that is supposed to be centuries-old, and he does not even utter a command. In fact, Barlow does not speak throughout the entire film. Furthermore, the physical appearance of the vampire is a direct rip-off of Max Schreck and Klaus Kinski's vampires from both the 1922 and 1979 versions of NOSFERATU. The monster's true intelligence is behind James Mason's character of Richard Straker, the vampire's keeper. The vampire sequences are indeed a bit cliche and thus ineffective, and David Soul's colorless performance as the film's hero indicates that television executives need to learn a lot more about casting. There are some gruesome moments of shock and suspense (as when James Mason throws actor Ed Flanders against a wall of piercing antlers in reminiscent of the attack scene on Martin Balsam in Alfred Hitchcock's PSYCHO), but these images of occasional thrills quickly fade as another moment of purposeless fear takes its place. SALEM'S LOT is not the tedious disaster that other King film adaptations have been, in fact, considering the constraints of network television, the film is more respectable than devastating. The strongest element of the film is indeed James Mason's bothersome performance as Richard Straker, delivering clever dialogue with a nasal sneer, as the actor often did. Mason is more the cunning and subtle villain, while Barlow is nothing more than a cheap devise used for cheap thrills. Had SALEM'S LOT been a theatrical effort, Hooper could have delivered a much more frightening product.

THIRST

Australian 1979

The premise of this stylish shocker revolves around a vampire cult that tries to brainwash actress Chantal Contouri, who plays the descendant of a distinguished vampire family (Dracula?), into becoming a baroness-vampire. However, the vampires depicted here are more refined. They obtain their nourishment under cover by hitting blood banks and hospitals instead of the traditional neck-biting way. The international community of vampires meet annually in a health farm. There, they drug humans and milk them for their blood as part of a spiritual ritual. The film is suspensefully directed by Ron Hardy and I recommend THIRST for viewing as an alternative to the traditional vampire film.

NIGHTWING

Columbia   1979

Based on the interesting novel by Cruz Smith, NIGHTWING is a film about a flock of deadly vampire bats that threaten an entire community. The film is tedious, mostly as a result of Arthur Hiller's direction . Hiller, who has a background in comedy, plays down any chance of horror in this film. The entire horror elements established early on in the film's premise diminish as we learn that the bats carry bubonic plague and that any mystical aspects of them being vampiric or flying demons called upon by a medicine man are false. The film also suffers from David Warner's abysmal performance as the vampire bat killer. However, special visual effects artist Carl Rambaldi has created some very good mechanical vampire bats for this science fiction- adventure film. I would say that director Frank Marshall achieved a better more thrilling rollercoaster effect with ARACHNOPHOBIA (1990), except the bats were replaced with spiders.

VAMPIRE

MTV   1979

Remarkably effective made for television film that actually surpasses SALEM'S LOT (1979) in quality shock scenes. The film presents all the standard trappings of a Gothic vampire film intelligently and convincingly in a modern day San Francisco setting. The cast is superb, as actors Jason Miller and E.G. Marshall stalk the vampire through the city streets. Richard Lynch, who normally portrays villains, appears quite comfortable as the central vampire figure who, in the film, is over eight hundred years old. Lynch's blonde vampire is ruthless, very cunning and reminiscent of David Peel's Baron Meinster in Hammer's BRIDES OF DRACULA (1960).

NOCTURNA (1979)

Compass International   1979

NOCTURNA plays the Dracula legend for laughs. Aging John Carradine and Yvonne DeCarlo play Count and Countess Dracula. Their lovely granddaughter (played by the film's producer, Nai Bonet) is taken in by disco dancing and stripping and falls in love with a mortal man (played by Tony Hamilton), who eventually turns her into a mortal like himself. Bonet's acting is poor, but Carradine and DeCarlo are great as old flames in this comedy spoof directed by Harry "Tampa" Hurwitz. In the same league as DRACULA: FATHER AND SON (1977) and MAMA DRACULA (1979).

MAMA DRACULA

Valisa Films 1979

A parody on the Countess Elizabeth " Dracula" Bathory genre directed by Boris Szulzinger. In the film, Mama Dracula, who always stays young by drinking the blood of young virgins, has two sons, Vlad and Lad. Lad is too shy to bite and the other is a gay dress designer. But Mama Dracula, played by Academy-award winning actress Louise Fletcher, runs a boutique to attract victims and she is not too shy to put the bite on them! Unlike centuries ago when she could just order out, she must now rely on her boutique and her two bumbling twins to attract the attention of young virtuous women, primarily actress Maria Schneider. English dialogue was added by Tony Hendra for a very limited American release to capitalize on the success of LOVE AT FIRST BITE (1979) and the Dracula movie craze of that year.

NOSFERATU THE VAMPIRE

German/Gaumont   1979

Intellectually directed by Werner Herzog, this color remake of the silent 1922 classic is elegant. Actor Klaus Kinski is accurately made up to look like Max Schreck's Count Orlock. Kinski is brilliant as the growling, groveling vampire. A creature powerless to resist his own bloodthirsty instincts. Unlike Frank Langella's Dracula, there are no admirable qualities in this vampire, who is driven by forces beyond his power. Kinski's portrayal of Dracula reflects a careful study of the remarkable and rat-like Count Orlock of the 1922 version. Actress Isabelle Adjani gives a stylish performance as Lucy Harker, who sacrifices her own life to destroy the vampire by the dawn's early light. But Herzog adds a new twist ending to the film. Jonathan Harker, who has also become one of the infected, rides off maniacally to carry out Dracula's doom to the rest of the world. NOSFERATU is an impressive portrait of rotting, decadence and evil, atmospherically photographed by Jorg Schmidt-Reitwein and directed in a slow subtle style unlike most of the fast-paced mechanizations of Hollywood. NOSFERATU is a <u>true</u> contemporary horror film, with no paralleling boundaries between straight forward horror and spoof. The film is simply horror. A must see for diehard vampire movie fans.

VAMPIRE HOOKERS

Capricorn Three   1979

Good old John Carradine returns to the screen as Count Dracula once more. In this erotic film, Dracula dispatches three of his sultriest succubi to prowl the night for human blood. The three vampires lure several not-so-innocent men to the graveyard to meet their doom. The film is also known as THE SENSUOUS VAMPIRES.

DRACULA   SUCKS

M.H.E.   1979

Director Philip Marshak presents porno star John Holmes as Count Dracula in this soft porn version of the legend. The opening dialogue is almost a word for word remake of Tod Browning's DRACULA (1931) with added sex and horrible jokes. Boy, if Bram Stoker was alive to see this!

LOVE AT FIRST BITE

AIP 1979

American International Pictures' spoof on the Dracula legend did big business at the box office. The film hilariously pokes fun at the legend from beginning to end and comedian-actor George Hamilton gives freshness to the character of Count Dracula. In the film, the Transylvanian vampire decides to move away from his boring motherland to twentieth century New York! Apparently, the Count wants to take a bite of that big apple! Once there, he and his servant Renfield (played by Arte Johnson) disrupt a funeral in a Harlem chapel, raid a local blood bank for food and dance up a storm in a disco frenzy with model Susan St. James. Hamilton cunningly romances her with hypnotic charm, while her former husband (played by Richard Benjamin), who is a relative of the famous Professor Van Helsing, tries to rid the Big Apple of this menace and save St. James from the vampire's clutches. Dracula wins and transforms his bride to be into one of the undead like himself and we are all very happy for them. The script's one liners are often good, and Hamilton is great as Dracula with a heavy Lugosi accent. Director Stan Dragoti paces this film much better than the previous Mel Brooks parody on the Frankenstein legend, YOUNG FRANKENSTEIN (1974).

THE CRAVING

Dalmata Films 1980

Paul Naschy returns as an older Waldemar Daninsky, Spain's werewolf at large. In this film written and directed by Jacinto Molina, Waldemar and his sidekick Countess Bathory (Silvia Aguilar) are executed for witchcraft. Once again, the film shifts to modern times, and grave-robbers yank the ever so valuable silver dagger from Waldemar's chest causing him to fully revive. A young female student of the occult drenches Bathory's casket with human blood causing her to return to her undead existence. Now you have another film in which Bathory vampirizes virgins while Waldemar chomps down on the locals. The

killings are more graphic than normal and there is even a scene in which the nude vampire takes a shower in the dripping blood from one of her strung-up victims. How's that for gore? The film cleverly combines the Gothic atmosphere and trappings of the previous Paul Naschy epics with 1980's splatter. THE CRAVING is also known as RETURN OF THE WOLFMAN.

I DESIRE

MTV 1982

A bizarre tale about a Los Angeles prostitute who turns out to be a female vampire who does her victims in while doing the dirty deed. Actor David Naughton (of AMERICAN WEREWOLF IN LONDON) suspects the glorified prostitute (played seductively by Barbara Stock) as being a vampire. There are several confrontations between the two foes, the final of which is staged in the vampiress's elaborate penthouse apartment-lair. The average film, directed by John Llewellyn Moxey, is mostly all bark and very little bite, but the contemporary setting holds up rather well, which says a lot for a television film.

THE HUNGER

MGM 1983

Catherine Deneuve plays a beautiful ageless vampire whose lovers share her immortality before growing old suddenly. The vampire, the last of a dying breed who live forever, lives in a Manhattan apartment and picks up her victims in a trendy disco nightclub. In the film's most incredible scene, actor David Bowie, who plays one of her pseudo-immortal mates, changes from youthful beauty to a nearly rotting corpse in just a single afternoon, all this is the result of one blissful night of decadent passion with the " black widow" Deneuve. In one of the film's better moments, Bowie tries to get gerontologist Susan Sarandon to stop his aging process before he crumbles away. He ages a hundred years while on hold in her waiting room. The film is stylish and very artistic at times, using

fluttering doves, shafts of sunlight, erotic lesbian sex, buckets of blood and the transfer of personalities from vampire Deneuve to her woman victim (played by Susan Sarandon) to create some type of nightmarish mood, however confusing it may all seem. THE HUNGER was made by Tony Scott, brother of accomplished filmmaker Ridley Scott and based on the novel by Whitley Strieber. However, the film suffers from Scott's background in television commercials and his lack of experience in motion pictures.

THE BLACK ROOM

Independent 1983

Incredibly fascinating low budget film directed by Norman Thaddeus Vane in which immortal brother and sister vampires (played by Stephen Knight and Cassandra Gavioa) are too nervous to take blood the traditional way. Instead, they rely on medical transfusions to keep their hereditary anaemia status cuoe. The siblings rent out a room in their Beverly Hills Mansion to a philandering couple. The husband uses the room to cheat on his wife, while the wife does a little cheating herself. With the help of his sister, the brother drains various visitors of their blood, which he needs to survive. There is a lot of blood spilling in this film during the transfusion scenes but the film is brilliantly photographed by Robert Harmon and is one of the better serious contemporary vampire films released during the 1980's.

THE TOMB

Trans World Entertainment 1985

"The Mummy Meets The Vampire!" cleverly describes the premise of this film. Fortune hunters desecrate an Egyptian tomb and must pay the price when the Egyptian princess Nefratis (Michelle Bauer) returns to life as an ancient-old vampire. THE TOMB , under the direction of Fred Olen Ray (director of BIOHAZARD of 1984; THE ALIENATOR of 1989), offers very generous amounts of blood and gore.

35

In fact, many of the original gory scenes had to be cut to achieve an R rating before it was released theatrically. THE TOMB is ideal for enthusiasts of splatter.

ONCE BITTEN
Columbia   1985

Jim Carrey plays a teenage male virgin whose looking for love in all the wrong places. Carrey's life goes haywire when he does the dirty deed with sexy, centuries-old female vampire Lauren Hutton, who has a need for young male virgins. What a combination? The film is an outright comedy along the lines of LOVE AT FIRST BITE (1979) and I WAS A TEENAGE VAMPIRE (1987), offering some very funny moments.

FRIGHT NIGHT
Columbia   1985

Tom Holland's trendy vampire thriller was originally intended to do for vampires what Rob Bottom's THE HOWLING (1981) did for werewolves. Unfortunately, the Holland film gets side-tracked and as a result, the film emerges as a Count Yorga-ish film illuminated with some jazzy special effects and some horrible adolescent comedy.   The film is more of a traditional vampire film than Tony Scott's more serious THE HUNGER (1983) and quite frankly, despite the doses of flat at times comedy and cliche dialogue, FRIGHT NIGHT is still very entertaining and spooky at times, especially for those viewing the film for the very first time. A young boy (played by William Ragsdale) notices activity in the once-abandoned house next door. After a series of shocking events, Ragsdale comes to the conclusion that his new neighbor, Jerry Dandridge (played by Christopher Sarandon) is a horrible vampire. In a desperate attempt to save his girlfriend, his mother, and his neighborhood, the young lad employs movie vampire hunter Christopher Vincent (played brilliantly by veteran actor Roddy McDowell) to help destroy the cunning vampire next door. What follows is a series of often predictable encounters between our heroes and the villains, some very flashy transformation scenes in which the vampire transforms into a horrendous mechanical vampire bat, and a few laughs and shocks. Instead of going straight for the throat with shock and atmosphere, the film plays for comedy and visual effects. Ken Diaz's special effects are great, but runs a tie against McDowell's exuberant performance as a cowardly vampire killer (he is the film's only fully developed character). Unfortunately FRIGHT NIGHT fails at accomplishing the fear that THE HOWLING delivers and cannot be compared, however the film is entertaining.

LIFE FORCE
Warner   1985

Based on the novel Space Vampires written by Colin Wilson, and originally planned under the same title, LIFE FORCE starts out as an outer space epic, then becomes a vampire yarn that turns into an end-of-the-world saga. A space probe leads an alien spacecraft to reach Earth from which three humanoid space vampires are released onto London. With just a kiss, they can actually drain the life force out of a single human body. Their victims are turned into mindless zombies who must then suck the life force from others. Controlling it all is a beautiful nude space vampiress. The premise is so ridiculous that certain moments of the film are actually unintentionally funny. Tobe Hooper's direction here is clearly a tribute to Hammer films. I cannot   help feel the similarities between the climax of LIFE FORCE and that of Hammer's FIVE MILLION YEARS TO EARTH (1968), in which London is totally devastated with mass destruction. The special effects of this film are better than the Hammer film, due to the revolutionary techniques developed since 1968, but unfortunately, not even the effects can save this film from its fate due to poor scripting and acting. I am afraid LIFEFORCE could have been a much better, more thrilling picture.

VAMP
New World   1986

In the same league as FRIGHT NIGHT is VAMP, an equally entertaining tale of modern-day vampires blended with the uncertain adolescent humor that usually accompanies such films. VAMP, directed by Richard Wenk, stars Grace Jones as Katrina, the sultry leader of a den of vampires who puts the bite on some college kids and who is also the owner of the After Dark Club, naturally located in the most seedy part of this big city.   The vampires dovetail with human society, using a strip joint as their cover to attract lonely men who are hardly likely to be missed. They are the vampires' perfect victims (as in the case of the film WOLFEN). Grace Jones is brilliant as the exotic and scary vampire leader who was once an Egyptian queen, but actor Chris Makepeace is unconvincing as the hero. The film takes place all in one night, and is therefore fast-paced. Makepeace and friends Robert Rusler and Gedde Watanabe venture into the seamy and derelict red-light district and into the After Dark Club in search of a stripper for their party. They soon fall prey to the alluring but fatal vampire strippers of the club. The vampires are slain by way of fire (ala the climax of THE HOWLING), bow and arrow and even the wooden heel of a pump! Grace's vampire is destroyed by sunlight when Makepeace corners her under the sewery catacombs of the city. Although many aspects of the film are unexplained, VAMP is actually superior at times to Tom Holland's FRIGHT NIGHT (1985) in creating the sensual moods of horror that are usually associated with vampire films. Advertisements for the film read "VAMP - It'll bite you dead!" and "The first kiss could be your last!" Great fun! In fact, Grace Jones should consider a sequel.

I MARRIED A VAMPIRE
Prism   Entertainment   1986

Another silly and mindless spoof on the vampire legend. In this film, Rachel Gordon plays Viola, a young voluptuous woman who runs away from her small town life style and her parents to the big city. The people prove to be very harsh and cold and her romantic notions of living in such a big city are shattered by its harshness and sleaziness. Her one great savior arrives when she unknowingly marries a vampire named Robespiere (Brendan Hickey). How ironic. But the twist works well. Poor Viola, the signs were not clear enough in the beginning: The groom wants a honeymoon in Transylvania and he sleeps in a king-size casket! Someone really needs to tell this woman to wake up! But somehow the fact that her husband is a vampire only helps her along in the big city. Together they share sweet love and happiness as they carry out sweet revenge on the low-life scum of the city. From the creators of the TOXIC AVENGER and NUKE 'EM HIGH, I MARRIED A VAMPIRE is written and directed by Jay Haskin in a similar fashion. "Till Death Do Us Part!" "A Vow They Won't Have To Keep!" Catchy advertising for a vampire film.

GRAVEYARD SHIFT

1987

Not to be confused with Ralph Singleton's 1990 Stephen King film of the same title. Gerard Ciccoritti's GRAVEYARD SHIFT deals with a vampiric member of a vampire harem in New York City. Our vampire hero is played by Silvio Oliviero, who, at three hundred and fifty years old, drives an all night cab as a clever and nonchalant device to obtain human blood. He soon becomes undone by his soft-heartedness when he betrays his coven-like harem of previous victims and settles down with a suicidal lady film director. The entire film is played out much like a bad dream, and is inferior in many ways to FRIGHT NIGHT (1985), VAMP (1986), THE LOST BOYS (1987) and NEAR DARK (1987), the latter of which was released in competition with GRAVEYARD SHIFT.

NEAR DARK

DEG   1987

Lance Henriksen leads a group of trashy American vampires who drift around the lonely Midwest highways, terrorizing redneck bars and sucking the blood out of cocky cowboys. The vampires are depicted as gypsies (not in the literal sense), constantly moving from one Midwest city to another. The film's premise of how these vampires dovetail with modern society begins when a female vampire bites a young man (Adrian Pasdar) on his neck. She does not "bleed" him, therefore this causes him to transform into one of the nocturnal creatures. The boy just does not have it in himself to kill for blood, but bad boy vampire Bill Paxton (ALIENS & PREDATOR II) teaches him how to prey on humans in several grisly sequences that will please the splatter enthusiast. As in his previous genre films, Paxton delivers his usual comedic lines. In one scene where he's about to bite a redneck victim in a cowboy bar, he comments, " I hate when they don't shave!" The film is not intended to be a comedy in any way, nor does it resemble one. But these lines have become common in modern horror films. NEAR DARK offers some interesting vampire trappings, such as when Pasdar, who is unable to kill a human for blood, sustains himself by feeding off his girlfriend's stolen blood. Unusual to the tradition is the method in which Pasdar's vampire becomes human again after his vampiric blood is drained and his father's blood is transfused into his body. He then becomes the film's savant and destroys the other vampires with the help of the sun's rays. The grisly tale is well mounted and features some great special effects. NEAR DARK, like VAMP, FRIGHT NIGHT and THE LOST BOYS, is one of the first of the new contemporary vampire films that emerged during the late 1980's and 1990's. Not bad!

THE LOST BOYS

1987

Joel Schumaker's big budget tale of teenage vampires reduces the vampire legend to "MTV meets the vampires!" Like FRIGHT NIGHT and VAMP before it, THE LOST BOYS deals with borderline horror and comedy, as a new family moves into a small California town and the oldest son is immediately taken with a local teenage girl who just happens to be a vampire. The coming out of our hero-turned vampire Jason Patric is handled in comic fashion, but the moments in which Patric must confront himself and the lead vampire (played by Kiefer Sutherland) along with his rat-pack-clan is played for cheap thrills and melodramatics. Schumaker does tease us with some very stylish scenes and some interesting vampire folklore, as well as a shocking twist ending. Corey Haim plays Jason Patric's brother and the film's teenage savant and Jami Gertz plays his teenage love interest, who wants desperately to be freed from Sutherland's restraints and her dreadful curse. The performances and dialogue are above average for this type of film and the vampire scenes are quite good. The film is pretty much similar to FRIGHT NIGHT and VAMP in context.

A RETURN TO SALEM'S LOT

Warner   1987

This film actually works as a dark comedy without the adolescent trappings of FRIGHT NIGHT and VAMP. Genre director Larry Cohen uses comedy as a dark device to relieve the shock effects of this film. For example, the vampires of this community prefer to drink the blood of farm animals, but an old grandma-like vampire who can't give up human blood complains that she has a "drinking problem!" Or the scene in which the central vampire figure of this film is impaled on the American flag! Michael Moriarty and his son return to their home town to find it infested with hundreds of vampires and demon creatures. The film's plot, also written by Cohen, is weakened by acts of senseless violence. I cannot help but describes this film as a cross between CHILDREN OF THE CORN (1985) and DAY OF THE DEAD (1985). The myths about garlic and reflections in mirrors are dispelled with this film and I must say, I was not very impressed with this sequel to SALEM'S LOT (1979).

MONSTER SQUAD
Vestron   1987

Universal's famous monsters rise from the dusty vaults to take back a magical amulet from a group of kids who call themselves the Monster Squad. The monsters, which include the Frankenstein Monster, the Wolfman and the Creature from The Black Lagoon are headed by Count Dracula (played by Duncan Regehr). Dracula wants the powerful amulet to rule the world. Naturally, the Monster Squad wins and saves the world from the domination of evil vampire. The name Alucard is even mentioned as part of the film's many nostalgic jokes written into the script by screenwriters Shane Black and Fred Dekker. The fast paced film directed by Dekker is surprisingly suspenseful at times and visually satisfying with some very astonishing atmospheric moments. I must say that it is great to see the old-style monsters return, especially Count Dracula!

VAMPIRE AT MIDNIGHT
New Age   1987

Gustav Vintas portrays vampire Victor Radkof, a new age hypnotherapist who finds himself falling for actress Lesley Miline. Jason Williams plays a cop investigating a string of vampire-style murders alongside the "good" doctor, who, to his horror, turns out to be the vampire responsible. The plot thickens when the savant competes with the monster for the same woman (Miline), and a battle to the finish ensues. Director Gregory McClatchy stylishly provides the film with clever plot twists, great special effects and some light gore to create a refreshing vampire tale.

NOT OF THIS EARTH
Miracle Pictures   1988

A pseudo-remake of the 1958 Roger Corman film that actually looks cheaper than the original. Arthur Roberts assumes the role of the alien vampire in dark shades who is transporting suitcases of human blood to his hungry planet. Former porn star Traci Lords plays the nurse who he hires to give him occasional blood transfusions, but it is she who catches onto his scam and brings about his downfall. The original Corman film was played straight, whereas this remake does offer an occasional laugh and snicker, primarily the gory scene in which one of the alien vampires goes on a murderous knife stabbing rampage when he is given the transfused blood of a rabid dog. There is no question about it, NOT OF THIS EARTH is definitely a bomb on every level, and if you ask me, I feel the Corman film is far superior in its subtleties than this picture directed by Jim Wynorski. The special effects by Alex Rambaldi are not up to par with that of the special effects techniques of his father Carlo Rambaldi.

THE   REJUVENATOR
Jewel Productions   1988

Released on video as REJUVENATRIX, this Brian Jones-directed, state-of-the-art horror film offers a unique twist to the vampire theme. Writers Simon Nuchtern and Brian Jones have come up with a premise in which scientist Dr. Gregory Ashton (John MacKay) develops an anti-aging formula from the brain cells of cadavers. He uses actress Elizabeth Warren (Vivian Lanko) as his guinea pig. We later learn that the effects of the serum are temporary, and larger doses are required to maintain youth and beauty. Soon Warren find herself attacking the living, killing them and eating their brains to stay young and beautiful. Director Jones uses state of the art special effects and enormous amounts of gore to raise the level of this film, but unfortunately, THE REJUVENATOR is just another splatter variation on the vampire legend and a cross between DEATH BECOMES HER (1992) and THE WASP WOMAN (1959).

DRACULA'S   WIDOW
DEG   1988

Director Christopher Coppola brings together Dracula's widow and the descendants of both Jonathan Harker and Dr. Van Helsing in this quite silly rehashing of the Dracula legend. Sylvia Kristel performs here as Dracula's sultry widow Vanessa. The premise, written by Chris Coppola and Kathryn Thomas, introduces us to a young Raymond Everett (Lenny Von Dohlen), the owner and operator of a house of horror wax museum. Raymond has an affection for old vampire movies, and his new exhibit, direct from Romania, is on the Dracula legend. For his new display, Raymond receives six large crates from Romania, one of which carries the body of Dracula's Widow! Immediately upon her revival, she goes on a killing spree, wiping out most of Hollywood in a blink of an eye, turning her victims into hamburger meat. She even turns young Raymond into her slave. The Van Helsing character in the film is played as an old cook by actor Stefan Schnabel, who, during the last quarter of the film, is transformed into a bloodsucker too! The violence is senseless, but graphic for all you lovers of splatter, and the dialogue is flat. Kristel's characterization of Dracula's Widow is flat-out horrible. Her strong Romanian accent is pretentious. She's a bitch of a vampire with a bad attitude. The vampire in this film is used solely as a device to create graphic killings, and without these sequences there would virtually be no film, since the characters are not interesting enough to carry the film. She really has no meaningful dialogue or sympathetic emotions. Kristel's vampire closely resembles Max Schreck's Count Orlock in NOSFERATU (1922). The vampire is destroyed by Raymond, her slave, who drives a wooden stake through her heart, thus releasing him from any chance of becoming a nocturnal creature of the night. DRACULA'S WIDOW is an amateurish attempt by Coppola to update the Dracula legend into modern times. The film falls flat on its face, and it's no wonder distributors bowed away from national theatrical distribution. DRACULA'S WIDOW is available on video, but honestly, I cannot recommend the film for viewing, unless, of course, you are thrilled by senseless gore.

FRIGHT NIGHT II

Columbia   1988

Roddy McDowell returns to the role of fearless vampire killer Peter Vincent in this sequel to FRIGHT NIGHT (1985). Although his dialogue is a bit cliche and predictable, the actor does deliver another credible performance as the vampire killer, but for him to do it in a third film would simply be too much. Columbia hired four writers, including director Tommy Lee Wallace, to come up with this film's feeble plot. The film starts off well with the seductive sister (Julie Carmen) of the vampire Jerry Dandridge, who was destroyed by William Ragsdale and McDowell in the first film. Carmen moves into a large mansion next to a college dormitory with her entourage which includes a den of vampires, a manimal creature (Jonathan Gries) and a Renfield-type servant (Russell Clark) who eats moths. The sultry vampiress is totally bent on revenge, but Ragsdale calls upon McDowell to aide him in the disintegration of the beast by using mirrors to reflect the sunlight. The film offers strong graphic scenes of blood, impalements and rotting bodies to achieve its horror. The film's most graphic scene is when the vampire's manimal-friend is killed and his tummy bursts open and buckets of bugs, maggots and creepy-crawlies emerge. The original film is far superior to this effort and it amazes me how four talented and experienced screenwriters cannot come up with something better. It is a shame that many of the modern horror films released today rely mostly upon flashy special effects and graphic effects to create horror rather than relying on the monsters themselves.

DANCE OF THE DAMNED

New Classics   1988

The title of this film suggests that if you are a dancer in a strip joint, you are damned for eternity and subject to becoming one of the undead's prey. Sound confusing? So is the Andy Ruben and Katt Shea Ruben screenplay for this film. The premise here is very bizarre and I must add very silly. A female stripper and erotic dancer named Jodi (played by Starr Andreeff) finds herself miserable and suicidal. According to the film, the vampire (Cyril O'Reilly), walking the streets one night, passes her strip joint. From the sidewalk he can sense Jodi's desire to die. He enters and offers her $1,000 to spend the rest of the night with him until dawn. She all to easily accepts, and soon discovers what he is. The vampire, whose name we really never know, finds himself falling in love with her, but towards the film's ambiguous conclusion, he tries to kill her when she wants out. She no longer wants to know the pleasures of his other-worldly existence. Does he die from exposure to the sun or doesn't he? Apparently director Katt Shea Ruben leaves the answer to our imagination. This contemporary vampire film gives the vampire the capability of seeing and hearing through solid objects. The vampire can also move at a speed that would make even The Flash envious. DANCE OF THE DAMNED is really not one of the better contemporary vampire flicks, but it certainly is not the worst. If anything, the film tries hard to develop its characters, which is an aspect of filmmaking that the filmmakers of most modern horror films fail to achieve.

VAMPIRE KNIGHTS

Filmtrust   1988

Advertised as "The vampire comedy of 1988," VAMPIRE KNIGHTS is far from the praises of its own advertisement. In fact, the film should have been advertised as "The most ridiculous vampire film of 1988!" The title of the film "Vampire Knights" refers to a gang of mortals devoted to extinguishing the vampire race on planet Earth. The Knights are fully committed to protecting mortals from the savage vampires in this film, who are committed to literally sucking their young male victims dry in the most erotic ways. The storyline concerns a young man who travels to a small town to visit his friend. There he discovers that the night life is more than he bargained for. There are inept plot twists, one of which reveals that only one of the Knights is a mortal. VAMPIRE KNIGHTS is much in the same vein as BUFFY- THE VAMPIRE SLAYER (1992) without the teen idols.

TO DIE FOR

Trimark Pictures   1988

Producer Barin Kumar's loose, post modern adaptation of Bram Stoker's Dracula directed by Deran Serafian. The film tells how real estate agent Sydney Walsh, she plays the film's Jonathan Harker and Mina characters all rolled into one, is sent to Vlad's (Brendan Hughes) new Beverly Hills home. Naturally, Vlad is taken in by her beauty, not to mention the fact that during the previous night they had a romantic encounter. Steve Bond plays Tom, another vampire and Vlad's archenemy (apparently, Vlad once stole his woman). Amanda Wyss is Lucy, who becomes Vlad's first victim and who becomes very foul as she descends into vampirism. I think they call it being vamped! In any case, the Leslie King script uses scenes directly from the Bram Stoker novel, such as when Vlad cuts his chest and offers his blood to Walsh. But for the most part, the vampire elements are new and often silly, as when the two vampires fight each other during the film's climax. Vlad's destruction is very similar to Paul Naschy's in COUNT DRACULA'S GREAT LOVE. Vlad commits suicide, walking into the sunlight and decomposing into ashes. Apparently, the vampire feels that his love for Walsh is "To Die For!" Sequel, TO DIE FOR II: SON OF DARKNESS (1991).

LAIR OF THE WHITE WORM

First Fright   1988

Ken Russell's bizarre mix of vampirism and underground horror that is truly funny at times. Like some of his other work, the film is a satire. Hugh Grant plays the Lord of D'Ampton manor and descendant of the man who killed the infamous D'Ampton worm. Amanda

Donahoe is the vampire guardian of the thing which has survived in an underground network of caverns. She has been sacrificing to her her god for years and intends to give Grant's girlfriend to the beast. The vampirella actually bites off the willy of a naked boy in this film. I would prefer to think that Ken Russell will not make a sequel to this film, but then again, everyone has their own taste.

THE UNDERSTUDY: GRAVEYARD SHIFT II

Cinema Ventures 1989

Not that the original GRAVEYARD SHIFT warrants a sequel, but here it is anyway. Here we have a vampire who actually dominates the set, get this, of a vampire movie in production. Director Gerard Ciccoritti, who also directed the original, pays homage to Carl Dryer's VAMPYR (1932) and Hammer's HORROR OF DRACULA (1958), which, because of this, gives the film a more familiar leg to stand on. In the film, the vampire (Silvio Oliviero) kills the leading man and promises the leading lady, Carmilla (Wendy Gazelle), an immortal life. So what's new? The premise, also written by Ciccoritti, does not really give us something unique and fresh, but the film is still worth a look for those who truly admire vampire films in general.

CARMILLA

Showtime Express 1989

Sheridan Le Fanu's classic horror tale about the beautiful and mysterious Carmilla and her vampiric control over a family in a secluded mansion is reset in the American South. Carmilla is played by Meg Tilly. As a victim of a coach accident, she is taken in by a family and befriended by Maria (Played by Ione Skye). It does not take the vampiress long to turn everyone in the household against each other, resulting in some deaths that the local authorities and doctors classify as part of some unknown plague. Roddy McDowell portrays Inspector Amos, who has different ideas. In the film he says, "The plague does not bite!" It is the Inspector who sets a trap to prove

Carmilla is a vampire, but he too meets his destiny when the vampire shoves a wooden stake through his mouth and head. Eventually, Carmilla is impaled during a struggle with Maria but this is after we learn that the beautiful young creature was involved with several other vampires, perhaps the Karnsteins? In accordance with tradition, CARMILLA offers some good atmospheric photography and lesbianism between the vampire and the victim. There is a fabulous but bizarre scene to look out for in which Carmilla is seen floating in thin air while she sucks Maria's neck for blood. Amazingly, the film, which runs approximately ninety-three minutes, is produced by Shelly Duval. Directed by Gabrielle Beaumont in a made-for-television style.

VAMPIRE'S KISS

Hemdale Film Corp 1989

To be or not to be? This is the question that still rings in my head after watching this very bizarre tale of vampirism and psychotic behavior. You are never really sure that the film's star, Nicholas (MOONSTRUCK) Cage is transforming into a creature of the night. The film flows ever so slowly and during its beginning seems very promising and faithful to the genre. Cage plays Peter Loew, a young business executive for a literary agency. Peter is frustrated because he cannot really find himself a steady girlfriend. He speaks his frustrations to his psychiatrist (Played by Elizabeth Ashely). It is one night that the mysterious and sultry Rachel (Jennifer Beals) comes into Peter's life. In a very impressive scene that we at first believe is actually occurring, Rachel sinks her fangs into Peter's neck. From this point forward the young executive begins to descend into madness as he believes that he is actually transforming into a vampire. Like Romero's MARTIN (1975), Peter even goes so far as to buy a pair of plastic Halloween vampire fangs and walk the streets of New York in a Max Schreck-type fashion harassing women at night clubs and screaming

out "I'm a vampire!" It soon becomes evident that Peter is suffering from his own emotional frustrations and the vampire persona he has adopted is a form of release of the pressure he is suffering from. Therefore, Rachel, the sultry vampiress is nothing more than a figment of his imagination. Better yet, Rachel is the creation of the dark side of his mind that eventually forces him to the point of murder. Even his own psychiatrist is a figment of his imagination, representing the good side of his inner self. Maria Conchito Alonso plays Alva, Peter's secretary and the true victim of Peter's madness. Through his descent, Alva is pushed too far and it is her brother who actually shoves a wooden stake through Peter's heart during the climax of this somewhat ambiguous film. Peter's fantasy is lived up to his last breathing moments. VAMPIRE'S KISS is by no means a faithful tale of vampirism, but the pseudo-supernatural elements featured in this film are surprisingly effective. Cage gives a wonderful performance that even Jack Nicholson would bow to and it is his performance that steals the show.

TRANSYLVANIAN TWIST

MGM 1989

In the great style of Mel Brook's YOUNG FRANKENSTEIN, TRANSYLVANIAN TWIST, a Roger Corman production directed by Jim Wynorski, is a spoof on the vampire and horror genres. In the film, Steve Altman accompanies pop star Teri Copley to her uncle Byron Orlock's castle in Transylvania. Orlock is played by actor Robert Vaughn, in his first and only performance as a bloodsucker. At the castle, Copley inadvertently locates her dead father's book of witchcraft. The film is abundant in horror jokes and cameos, one of which includes the late Boris Karloff (via clips from his film THE TERROR). Most of the horror and supernatural elements are predictable and played for laughs. MONSTER SQUAD (1987) is superior if you love monsters and a giggle.

VAMPIRE COP

Panorama Entertainment 1990

From the director of such blood feasts as CANNIBAL HOOKERS (1987) and DEMON QUEEN (1986) comes this Don Farmer vampire tale full of gushing gore and unnecessary violence. The premise, in which the vampire once again dovetails with society, is quite clever. During the daylight hours he sleeps upside down in his apartment, but an night, the central vampire hides behind the badge, infecting local drug dealers, who would otherwise go uncared for. As mentioned earlier, there are many gory moments, most of which are uncalled for, and the traditional vampire trappings are second best to the graphic action.

I BOUGHT A VAMPIRE MOTORCYCLE

Hobo Films 1990

Are you ready for this one? A motorcycle that drinks human blood? What will Hollywood think of next? A man buys a motorcycle and soon after he discovers that the bike will not take gas. Instead it prefers human blood. Soon, the poor guy begins to find his friends dead, drained of all their blood. You'd think these incidents would have alerted him, but no! For God sake, the bike will only start at night! I would recon to say that this film is the poorest and most inept conception for a vampire film that I have ever seen. If you love camp and cheap thrills, this is your film. Whatever happened to those good old fashion Hammer vampire films that you could really sink your teeth into?

RED BLOODED AMERICAN GIRL

Prism 1990

The AIDS scare comes around full effect in this bizarre and campy vampire tale directed by David Blyth. The film is actually like David Cronenberg's RABID (197?) in that the premise tries to combine science with this traditional disease or curse known as vampirism. Actor Christopher Plummer plays a scientist who dabbles with colleague Andrew Stevens in their development of drugs. Plummer is working on a new drug that will cure AIDS by way of an addictive virus that actually causes people to desire human blood. Before you know it, everyone in this film becomes addicted, including Plummer himself, who claims, "Yes, I'm a blood user, but I love garlic and hate sleeping in coffins!" Heather Thomas plays a clinic volunteer who gets bitten by a blood lust infected inmate, and soon she goes on a blood craved rampage, cutting people's toes open and taking claim to the title character.

THE HOWLING VI: THE FREAKS

Allied Productions 1991

"Vampire vs. Werewolf, The Ultimate Clash of the Forces of Evil!" read the advertisements for this routine contemporary werewolf film. THE HOWLING VI revolves mainly around a carnival of sideshow freaks commanded by a vampire named Harker, who is played by British actor Bruce Martyn Payne. The vampire in this film is mostly nocturnal, with long blonde hair and a sneering accent. He is hardly convincing and he is barely tolerable, but he is unquestionably sinister. Actor Brendan Hughes (TO DIE FOR) plays the film's new werewolf, who is first conceived as the evil monster responsible for slaying the inhabitants of a small American town. He is ridiculously captured by the vampire and displayed in his circus of freaks as an oddity. Naturally, the premise leads to that ultimate battle in which the werewolf becomes the hero and slays the vampire by driving a metal spike into his throat. To add excitement to this otherwise dull film, the werewolf dramatically leaps onto a curtain and shreds it with his claws, allowing the sun to burst through the window and onto the vampire. The sun's rays literally roasts the vampire to ashes. The special effects do not rise near the excellence of the original Howling film and Kevin Rock's screenplay does not deliver nothing near an original concept. The film does offer some satisfying moments of shock, and the opening scene is orchestrated nicely by director Hope Perello. But with a larger budget and a sharper script, the film could have been much better; which is usually the case with most of these films. I am sure there will be a HOWLING VII, no doubt!???

I WAS A TEENAGE VAMPIRE

New World 1990

First there was TEEN WOLF and TEEN WOLF II and before that I WAS A TEENAGE WEREWOLF, I WAS A TEENAGE FRANKENSTEIN and BLOOD OF DRACULA. Now comes this horrible, low budget film about teenage adolescence and vampirism. Young Murphy Gilcrease is the giek and laughing stock of the class. He's totally uncool, until one night he visits Jo-Dan's Motel and local whore house. There he becomes the victim of a vampiric prostitute. He soon finds his instant ticket to the cool life as he descends into vampirism. With his leather jacket, dark sunglasses and his super-human strength, he becomes the envy of his entire high school. Bullies shy away from him and delicious blondes find him irresistible. But honestly, the entire film is so bad. Writer-director Samuel Bradford uses cheap comedy lines such as when Murphy's mother discovers her son's fangs for the first time and comments, "I'll have to take you to the orthodontist." The comedy elements and the vampire trappings are just so bad that they really hinder what already is an unsalvable film. Released on video as TEEN VAMP for those who dare to sit through eighty-seven minutes of adolescent vampire mayhem. BUFFY THE VAMPIRE SLAYER is much better, if you can believe?

NIGHTLIFE

USA Television 1990

Writer - director Daniel Taplitz and writer Anne Beatts have cleverly combined comedy and horror to make what is one of the better post-1980 vampire films. In fact, the film is at times far superior to FRIGHT NIGHT (1985) and VAMP (1986), both of which try harder than the other to successfully combine horror with light comedy. Both films fail due to the adolescent nature of the comedy contents while NIGHTLIFE succeeds because the comedy, although a bit cliche at times, work well because it is well written and used properly. You know you are in for a good witty film when the opening credits cuts from one skeletal remain to another while the soundtrack to the song " I Don't Get Around Anymore" plays in the background. The film is set in Mexico, and the graves of one hundred year old mummies are being unearthed. Uncovering one of the coffins, two Mexican grave-diggers reveal the fresh, undecomposed body of Angelique (Maryam D'Abo), a beautiful vampiress who buried herself alive for one hundred years to hide from her evil and wicked master Vlad (Ben Cross of the new DARK SHADOWS television mini-series that aired in 1991). It is uncertain weather Cross's Vlad is actually Dracula. The screenwriters lead us to believe that he could possibly be the infamous Count, but this is never mentioned. Her discovery is publicized and Vlad is soon in Mexico in search of his lost love. Meanwhile Angelique falls in love with her doctor David (Keith Szarabajka), who falls in love with her blood condition (how ironic!). With the help of her doctor, Angelique realizes that she does not have to kill for blood. Surprise honey, there are blood banks in the modern world! This does not change Vlad's nature to kill for blood. But this film would not be half as good as it is had there been no complications, such as when we learn that the blood transfusions cannot control Angelique's virus. The transfusions of regular blood are just like drinking a bloody mary without the vodka! The concept introduced here is that the vampire scares its victim first, which creates a certain chemical that is released into the bloodstream which in turn keeps the vampire alive. The climax is staged in a Gothic castle where Vlad is staked in the heart. However, director Taplitz closes the film with a hint that there will be a sequel. One thing is certain, Taplitz maintains a happy medium between

horror and comedy, and there are some great atmospheric scenes from cinematographer Peter Fernberger. The script offers some great comic dialogue such as "Give me a lite. A blood lite!" and "Whatever you do, don't ever bury yourself alive!" Finally, the film ends with the soundtrack of the song, "I'll put a spell on you!" I must say, NIGHTLIFE is a refreshing variation on the traditional vampire theme. I fully recommend this film for viewing.

TO DIE FOR II: SON OF DARKNESS

Trimark Productions   1991

I thoroughly enjoyed this sequel to TO DIE FOR (1988), much more than the original film. Returning to the sequel are actors Steve Bond, Amanda Wyss and Scott Jacoby. Basically, the film tells how Count Vlad Tepish (Michael Praed) opens up a hospital in Los Angeles where he dispenses blood plasma to vampires Amanda Wyss and Steve Bond. While in Los Angeles, Vlad assumes the name of Max Schreck. Now Praed's handsome vampire is not the bloodthirsty fiend that his brother Tom (Bond) really is. In fact, Tom would like nothing more than to have his brother completely out of his way. He soon learns that Max is the father of Rosalind Allen's infant Tyler. In control of his co-vampire Cellia (Wyss), Tom dispatches her to go after Nina's (Allen) brother. We also learn that Nina does not know who the baby's real parents are; Tyler is adopted. There is also a good vampire named Jane, who aides the film's Van Helsing character Martin (Scott Jacoby) in locating the vampires' lair. Learning of her deceit, Tom captures Jane and ruthlessly handcuffs her to a large tree where she agonizingly perishes at sun rise. Tom really gets a kick out of this! Actually, Tom really gets a kick out of killing period! Everything moves at a predictable direction and at a steady pace. The film is so well made with good atmospheric photography for a contemporary setting, that it does not matter how predictable the Leslie King script really is. There are some great

love scenes between Vlad and the heroine mixed in with moderate gore for effect. The film concludes with a colossal battle between the two vampire brothers resulting in the staking of Tom, the decapitation of Nina's brother, and the destruction of Cellia. Finally, only Max remains, and as he is about to convince Nina to turn herself and Tyler over to the "dark side," Martin impales the beast with a stake. Max yanks the stake out and commands, "You think you are a match for me?" Just then, Martin leaps towards the curtains, ripping them down and allowing the sun to shower through. In an elaborate special effects scene, the vampire disintegrates. But what will happen to little Tyler? A sequel, perhaps? Director David F. Price proves that he can create quality horror material. I must say that out of all the modern-day vampire flicks, this one is actually superior, offering good performances, strong atmospheric photography and a good original music score by Mark McKenzie.

VAMPYRE

Panorama Entertainment   1991

Producer - director Bruce G. Hallenbeck pays homage to Carl T. Dreyer's VAMPYR (1932) and many of the Hammer vampire films. In his attempt in creating something original, Hallenbeck's film becomes a bit unfocused and baffling at times. VAMPYRE suffers from many weaknesses beginning with poor performances, unconvincing characters, and, most obvious, insufficient funds. There are a couple moments in which the film appears professionally made, rising above the troublesome capital crunch, but for the most part, VAMPYRE cannot achieve the grandeur it strives for. John Waters plays the film's hero, while Cathy Seyler is the voluptuous vampire woman reminiscent of those sultry Hammer vampires, who throws away her Hammer outfit and slips into a kinky leather gear. Wow!

SUBSPECIES

Full Moon - Paramount   1991

Don't let the commercial title fool you into thinking that this film is just another commercial splatter entry into the vampire genre. On the contrary. SUBSPECIES, while never reaching the quality of DRACULA (1979), the film remains one of the better, well-mounted contemporary vampire films made, which says a lot for this Charles Band production. Director Ted Nicolau maintains a contemporary setting while creating a Gothic atmosphere; the film's Transylvanian setting and architecture have a lot to do with the mood. The premise revolves around Transylvanian folklore and customs, and opens in a Gothic medieval castle wherein King Vladimir (Played by contemporary horror star Angus Scrimm) drinks the blood from the legendary bloodstone. According to the folklore, this stone drips the blood of saints and keeps the vampires from preying on humans for fresh blood. Of course, there's always one bad apple in every family, and in this case it is Radu (Anders Hove), the King's first born son, and an incredibly hideous, foul-looking creature of the night with two elongated fangs at the center of his mouth and claws that will slice a piece of steel (Radu was obviously created in the image of Count Orlock from the 1922 film NOSFERATU as a direct intention of projecting evil at its most undesirable). Radu kills his good-hearted father-vampire-King, and soon turns two young and beautiful American tourists (Laura Tate and Michelle McBridge) and their Transylvanian friend (Irina Movila) into his next victims. Radu succeeds into transforming both McBridge and Movila into foul vampires, but he is stopped in his tracks when he goes after Tate by his more handsome and kind-spirited half brother Stefan (Michael Watson). Stefan is nothing like the monster his brother is. The film ends with a nicely staged battle between the brothers resulting in the impaling and decapitation of Radu and the slaying of the vampire girls. Interestingly, Tate offers herself to Stefan, and together they live eternally happy as vampires. SUBSPECIES offers some great eerie

moments, as when Radu creeps his way through the corridors of a Gothic structure and begins to drink the blood from the wrist of his victim and then proceeds to suck the blood from her nipple. There is another equally effective and eerie scene in which one of the vampirized girls rises from her grave under the spell of Radu. The film is loaded with many of the familiar vampire trappings and folklore, and is far from boring. I think the marvelous special effects have a part in keeping the viewer's interest.

CHILDREN OF THE NIGHT

Fangoria Films   1991

From Fangoria's own publishers Norman and Steven Jacobs comes this unusual tale of modern vampirism; and who else but this team can tackle such a project better? The film is directed by Tony "HELLRAISER II" Randel, and stars Karen Black and Peter DeLuise. The premise by Christopher Webster and Nicolas Falacci is a refreshing switch from the traditional vampire film. The film is set in a small Midwest town. There, beneath the small town church sets a secret underground crypt where master vampire Czakyr (David Sawyer) resides. To get to this crypt, you must swim underwater through taverns. The town's children are kept underwater in suspended animation, eventually to be fed upon by Czakyr. Karen Black and Maya McLaughlin play mother and daughter vampires and Peter DeLuise is the visiting teacher sent to free the village from the evil vampire's hold. The film is okay stuff, but suffers from improper editing and poorly constructed time sequences. Like SALEM'S LOT (1979), the townspeople are one by one turned into vampires, and in that respect offers nothing original. However, the idea of the vampire's lair being subterranean is cleverly conceived. There are some good atmospheric moments worthy of some of the better vampire films. It is unfortunate that CHILDREN OF THE NIGHT never received theatrical distribution by Columbia. The film is available on video.

VAMPIRE HUNTER D

Epic/Sony & CBS   1992

Imaginative Japanese-made animated feature directed by Toyoo Ashida in which Hero D turns out to be a human vampire composite who hunts an evil race of vampires led by Count Magnus Lee and his beautiful daughter Anneka. The count and his daughter are revealed as descendants of the infamous Count Dracula. The film's climax has Anneka stressing her nobility, choosing to end her family's line rather than tolerate the count's mating with commoners. Ashida animates this feature with gory gusto and brief nudity. Most impressive are the backdrops and action sequences. The animated feature was originally produced and released in Japan in 1985 as HERO D - VAMPIRE HUNTER and released here in the United States in 1992 by Streamline Pictures. Will there be a Godzilla vampire film next? Just kidding!

A VAMPIRE IN PARADISE

Auramax   1992

Released in France in July of 1992 and in America in October 1992, this French-made film is an offbeat, cross cultural comedy with a tinge of mysticism. The story, written by Abdelkrim Bahoul, who also directed, tells of how an escaped lunatic who thinks he is a vampire perches himself cloaked in a cape outside a young girl's window. The man goes by the name of Nosfer Abi (Farid Chopel). With his ideal sunk-in features and cape, Nosfer Abi runs around Paris as a Nosferatu sinking his fangs into innocent people in hopes that he will be killed (Sound familiar? Nicholas Cage in VAMPIRE'S KISS of 1989). Soon the young French girl (Laure Marsac) perturbs her parents when she begins throwing random fits in Arabic. What follows is offbeat mixture of comedy and the supernatural as the parents send for an African exorcist to visit their home. Like VAMPIRE'S KISS (1989), A VAMPIRE IN PARADISE pokes fun at notions of sanity and insanity and the pseudo vampire and supernatural

43

elements are used to unite two youths from different cultures.

BUFFY THE VAMPIRE SLAYER

20th Century Fox 1992

Compared to Columbia's FRIGHT NIGHT (1985) and other horror-comedy vampire films such as VAMP and LOST BOYS, BUFFY THE VAMPIRE SLAYER is flat and humorless. The film, produced and directed by Fran Rubel Kuzui, is technically bargain basement material aimed at the masses and diehard fans of Beverly Hills 90210. The film's central character is of course Buffy (played by Kristy Swanson), lead cheer leader and voted Miss Popular at Hemery High School in San Fernando Valley. Just as vampires live eternally, so, apparently, do female vampire slayers. A dirty old man in a long overcoat named Merrick (Donald Sutherland) turns up to inform Buffy that she is one of these rare breed. He requests that she accompany him to the graveyard where she passes her first trial as a vampire slayer. Merrick trains Buffy in preparation of combatting actor Rutger Hauer as vampire King Lathos, who is planning a full scale invasion of Los Angeles with the aide of his vampiric thugs. Actor Luke Perry plays Buffy's boyfriend Pike, who is also menaced by the vampire clan. The vampires crash a high school dance in flashback of CARRIE, but during the climax the undead creatures of the night are vanquished by Buffy. Unfortunately, Sutherland and Hauer, usually two great performers, are colorless and the comedy in Joss Whedon's script is flat, relying on Buffy's air-headed clique to constitute the main source of laughs. The seven million dollar production will undoubtedly make a profit because of Fox's vigorous ad campaign, but will BUFFY THE VAMPIRE SLAYER warrant a sequel? In any event, the film is much better than the travesty I WAS A TEENAGE VAMPIRE (1990) and DANCE OF THE DAMNED (1988), but certainly not a fitting contender in the vampire boom of the early 1990's, especially against a film like Francis Ford Coppola's BRAM STOKER'S DRACULA (1992).

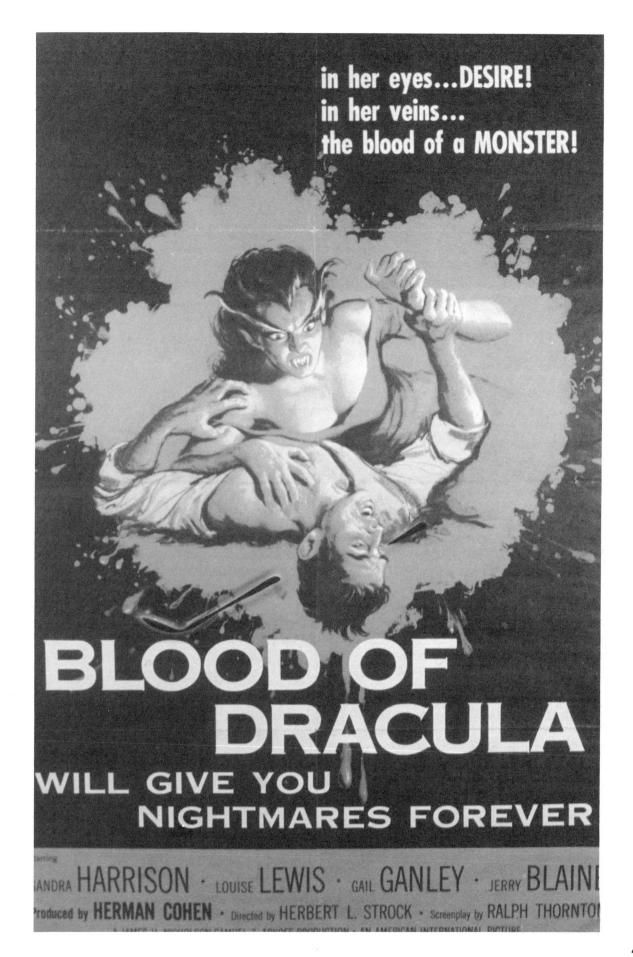

Lon Chaney, Sr. was the screen's first true horror star. He also became cinema's first master vampire. *Opposite* and *Above:* Lon Chaney as the psuedo-vampire in Tod Browning's silent masterpiece *LONDON AFTER MIDNIGHT* (1927).

48

Bela Lugosi is regarded as the legendary actor most associated with the character of Count Dracula. He is the epitome of the classic-style vampire. Opposite: Lugosi in his greatest role in DRACULA (1931). Top: Lugosi as the psuedo-vampire Count Mora in Tod Browning's MARK OF THE VAMPIRE (1935).

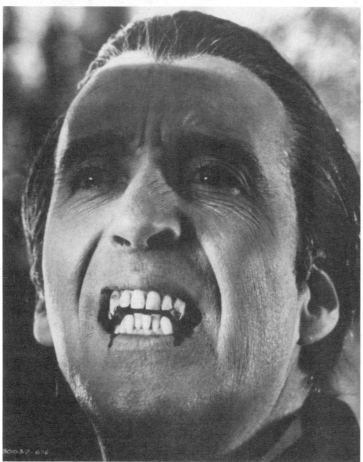

British actor Christopher Lee has portrayed the character of Count Dracula on the screen over seven times. Top: The actor made his debut as the Count in Hammer's HORROR OF DRACULA (1958), a contemporary masterpiece; Left: Lee's Dracula was tall, handsome, sinister, cunning and fanged as seen in this still from TASTE THE BLOOD OF DRACULA (1969); Opposite: Lee as the vampiric Count in DRACULA-PRINCE OF DARKNESS (1965).

The female species of the vampire race are equally lethal to the male species. *Opposite Top Left:* Ingrid Pitt gives a fang-tastic performance as Mircalla the vampire in Hammer's *THE VAMPIRE LOVERS* (1970); *Opposite Top Right:* Amanda Bearse shows us what she's made of in *FRIGHT NIGHT* (1985); *Opposite Bottom:* Ralph Bates discovers how deadly his girlfriend really is in *LUST FOR A VAMPIRE* (1971); *Top:* Ingrid Pitt bares her bloody fangs in *THE HOUSE THAT DRIPPED BLOOD* (1970); *Right:* The lethal vampiress from *THE VAMPIRE'S LOVER* (1961).

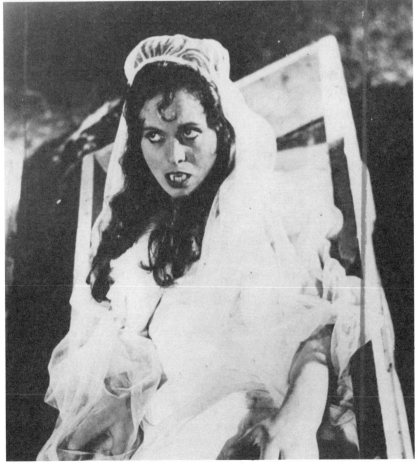

54

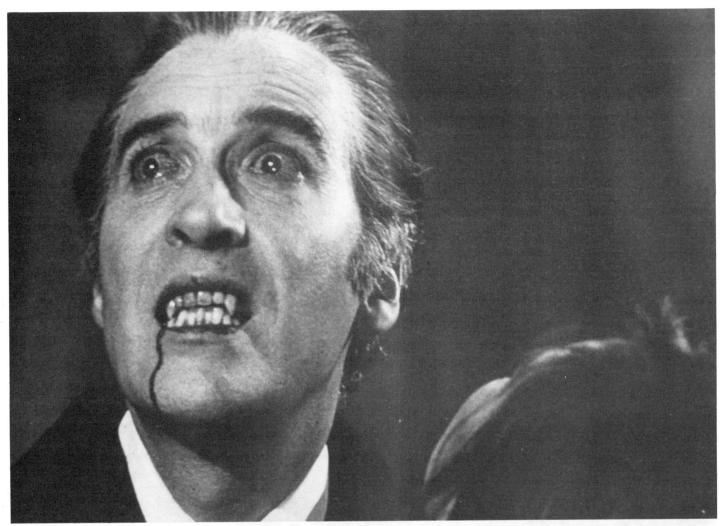

The vampire's bite is often sensual but always deadly. Opposite Top Left: Christopher Lee puts the bite on a lovely female victim in TASTE THE BLOOD OF DRACULA (1969); Opposite Top Right: The vampire prepares to take a bite in MARK OF THE WOLFMAN (1968); Opposite Bottom: A blood feast from VAMPIRE CIRCUS (1971); Top: Christopher Lee rejoices as he tastes the blood from Caroline Munro's neck in DRACULA A.D. – 1972 (1971); Right: Dracula's fangs penetrate the victim's flesh in this climatic scene from NOSFERATU (1979).

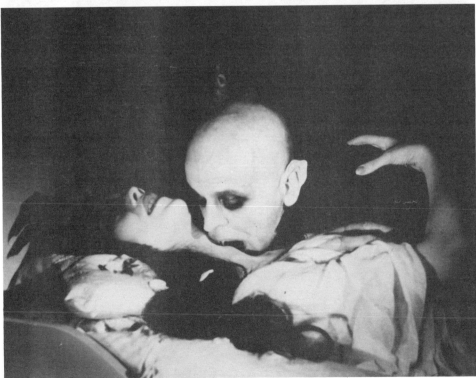

When faced with their own death, the vampire can become very lethal and savage. Opposite Top Left: The face of an angry vampire Kiefer Sutherland in THE LOST BOYS (1987); Opposite Top Right: Christopher Lee goes on a rampage when his plans go up in flames in THE SATANIC RITES OF DRACULA (1973); Opposite Bottom: Christopher Lee displays his rage once again in TASTE THE BLOOD OF DRACULA (1969); Top: William Marshall proves that he does not like to be threatened with the potential of death in BLACULA (1971); Right: The female vampire can also become dangerous when her life is threatened as seen in this still from HOUSE OF DARK SHADOWS (1970).

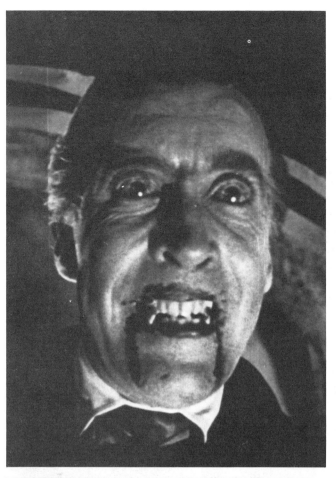 

 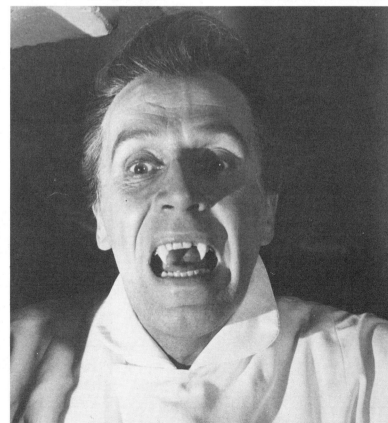

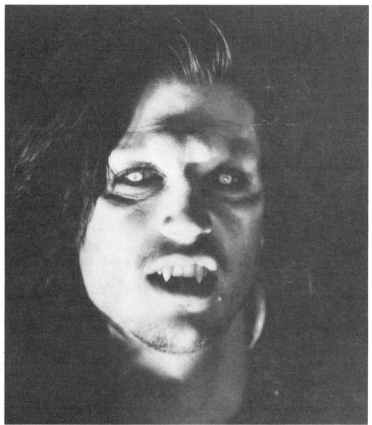

The vampire at close range is a very frightening sight. *Opposite Top Left:* Christopher Lee bares his bloody fangs in *HORROR OF DRACULA* (1958); *Opposite Top Left:* Barnabas Collins from *HOUSE OF DARK SHADOWS* (1970); *Opposite Bottom Left:* Bela Lugosi as the mysterious Count Dracula in *DRACULA* (1931); *Opposite Bottom Right:* Noel Willman as Count Ravna in *KISS OF THE VAMPIRE* (1963); *Top Left:* Barlow the vampire from *SALEM'S LOT* (1979); *Top Right:* One of the lost souls from *THE LOST BOYS* (1987); *Right:* The blood-hungry vampire from *BLOOD FOR DRACULA* (1973), also known as *ANDY WARHOL'S DRACULA.*

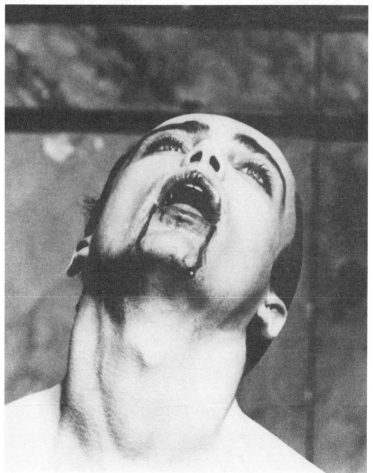

While the image of the vampire has changed over the past seventy years, the image of Count Dracula has virtualy remained consistent over the years, with a few alterations (blood, violence, fangs and gore). Opposite Top Left: Bela Lugosi as the classic Count Dracula in DRACULA (1931); Opposite Top Right: John Carradine as a slightly older and traditional Dracula in BILLY THE KID VS. DRACULA (1966); Opposite Bottom Left: Michael Pataki as Dracula in DRACULA'S DOG (1975); Opposite Bottom Right: Frank Langella as the handsome and very devious Count Dracula in DRACULA (1979); Top Left: Duncan Regher plays Count Dracula in THE MONSTER SQUAD (1987); Top Right: Christopher Lee bares his fangs as Dracula in TASTE THE BLOOD OF DRACULA (1969); Right: Klaus Kinski delivers a marvelous characterization of Count Dracula in NOSFERATU (1979).

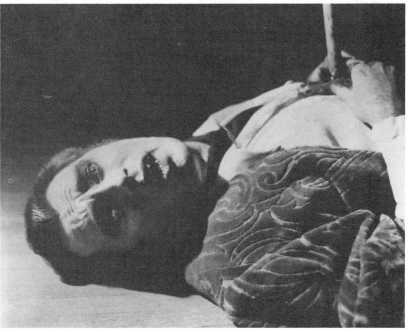

Death of a vampire by way of a wooden stake is usually not a pretty sight to behold, as illustrated in the following photos. Top: Christopher Lee is impaled with a wooden spoke during the opening scene of DRACULA A.D. - 1972 (1971); Left: Count Yorga is killed when he is staked with a wooden broomstick in COUNT YORGA - VAMPIRE (1970); Opposite Top: Vampiress Barbara Shelley is staked during a dramatic moment from DRACULA - PRINCE OF DARKNESS (1965); Opposite Bottom: Hammer's greatest stake-in-the-heart scene in which actor Christopher Lee gets the shaft in DRACULA HAS RISEN FROM THE GRAVE (1968).

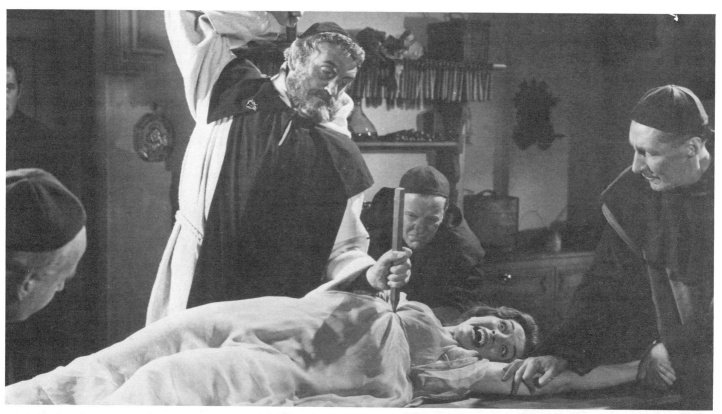

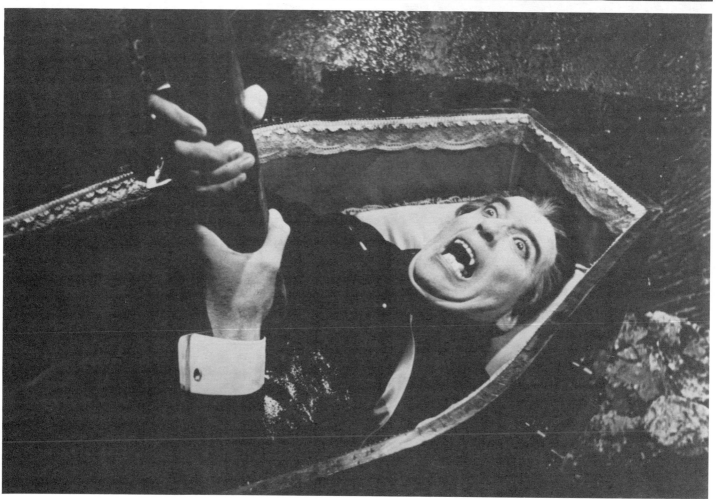

The crucifix and the vampire simply do not mix. Top: Count Alucard (Lon Chaney, Jr.) comes face to face with the mighty cross in SON OF DRACULA (1943); Left: Christopher Lee is handicapped by the powers of the crucifix in HORROR OF DRACULA (1958); Opposite Top: The cross proves to be no match for Frank Langella in DRACULA (1979); Opposite Bottom Left: The method of keeping a vampire at bay by wielding a crucifix is demonstrated by Roddy McDowell and William Ragsdale in FRIGHT NIGHT (1985); Opposite Bottom Right: Edward Van Sloan gives Bela Lugosi a good fright in DRACULA (1931).

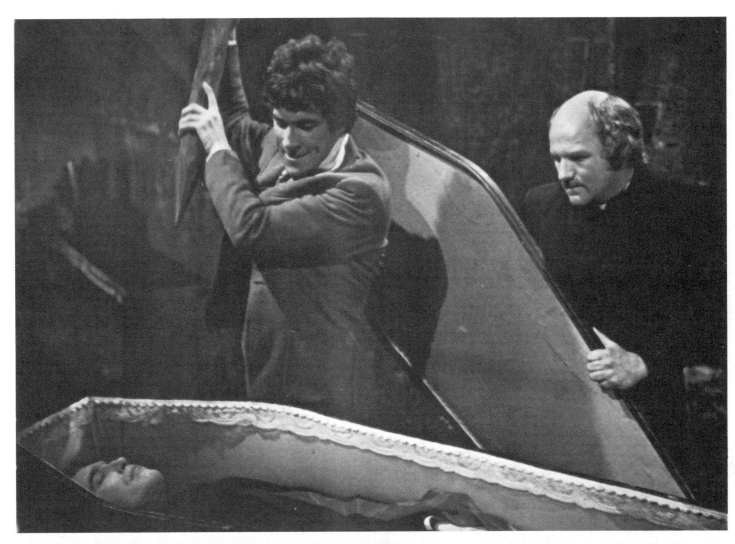

The vampire hunter is an integral part of the vampire film. Opposite Top: from DRACULA HAS RISEN FROM THE GRAVE (1968); Opposite Bottom: from BRAM STOKER'S DRACULA (1992); Top: from MARK OF THE VAMPIRE (1935); Above: from DRACULA (1979); Right: from HORROR OF DRACULA (1958).

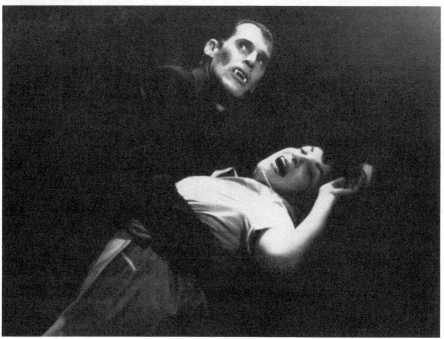

Drinking human blood is an age-old tradition with vampires. Top: Vampire Udo Kier drinks the blood of a female in Andy Warhol's BLOOD FOR DRACULA (1973); Left: Evil vampire Vlad (Ben Cross) prepares to drain the blood of a victim in NIGHTLIFE (1990); Opposite: Vampiress Julie Carmen prepares to sink her fangs for blood in FRIGHT NIGHT II (1988);

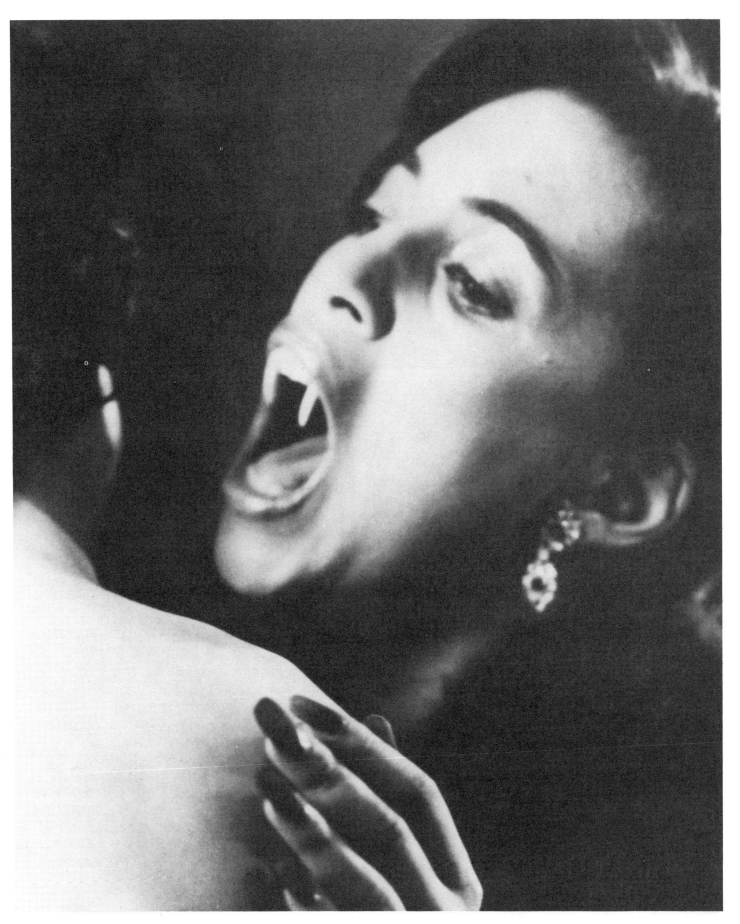

The vintage vampire is very different from the modern species. Top: This scene from Universal's SON OF DRACULA (1943) displays a good example of the vintage female vampire; Left: Bela Lugosi is the epitome of the classic screen Dracula in DRACULA (1931); Above: Carlos Villarias was the vintage Spanish-speaking Count Dracula in DRACULA (1931-Spanish version); Opposite Top: Lon Chaney, Jr. is a perfect example of the 1940's vampire in this publicity still from SON OF DRACULA (1943); Opposite Bottom: The classic-look of the 1930's vampire spread to Mexico, as evident in this scene from THE VAMPIRO'S COFFIN (1957).

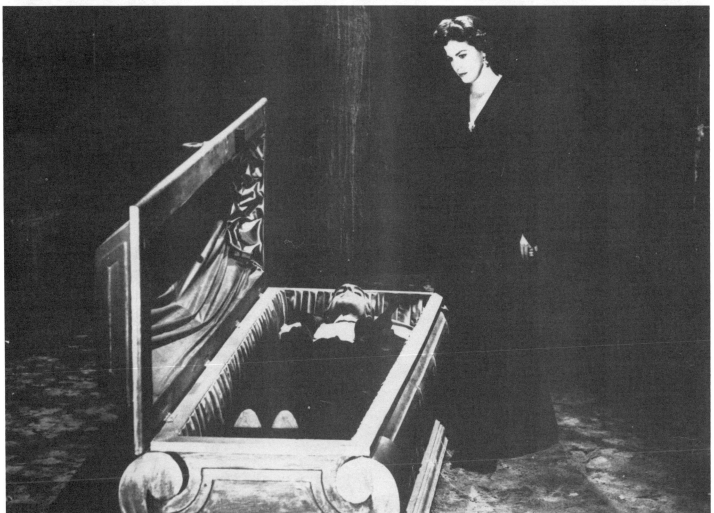

The master vampire has the ability to
lurk about in the dark undetected by
mortals. Vampires possess the power
to climb up the side of buildings and
find their way into your home.
Opposite Top: Vampire hunter Roddy
McDowell is totally unaware that
vampire Chris Sarandon is lurking just
outside the window in FRIGHT NIGHT
(1985); Opposite Bottom: Count
Orlock emerges from his hiding place
located on a large ship in NOSFERATU
(1922); Top: Count Dracula (Frank
Langella) climbs down the side of a
building in this remarkable scene from
DRACULA (1979); Right: Christopher
Lee's Dracula finds his way into the
house of his victim in this creepy
scene from Hammer's DRACULA –
PRINCE OF DARKNESS (1965).

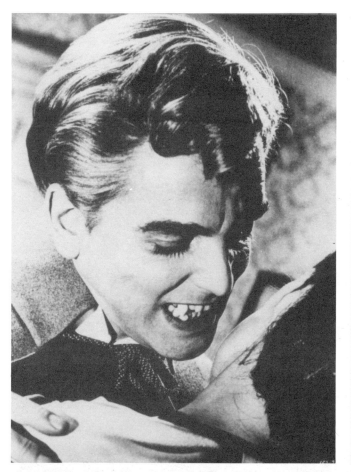

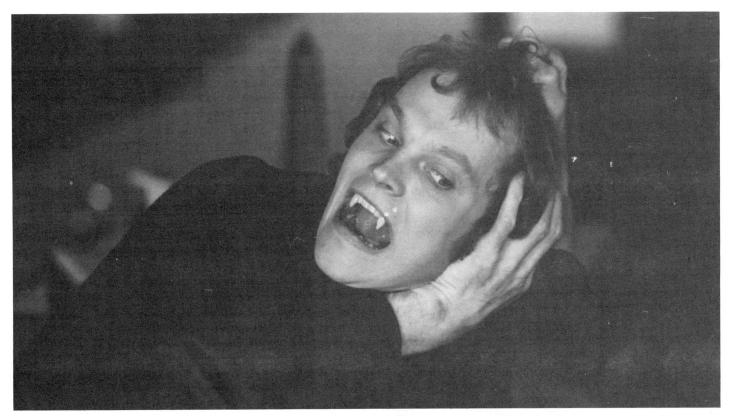

The vampires of Hammer Studios are legendary. Hammer introduced a new colorful vampire that literaly made the traditional-style vampire introduced by Bela Lugosi completely obsolete. Opposite Top Left: David Peel as the vampiric Baron Meinster in Hammer's BRIDES OF DRACULA (1960); Opposite Top Right: Ingrid Pitt as Countess Elizabeth Bathory emerges from her fountain of youthful blood in COUNTESS DRACULA (1970); Opposite Bottom: John Forbes-Robertson as Count Dracula in THE LEGEND OF THE SEVEN GOLDEN VAMPIRES (1973); Top: Christopher Neame as a lethal vampire disciple in DRACULA A.D. - 1972 (1971); Right: Christopher Lee is undoubtedly the greatest of the Hammer vampires. In this still, he portrays Dracula in Hammer's masterpiece, HORROR OF DRACULA (1958).

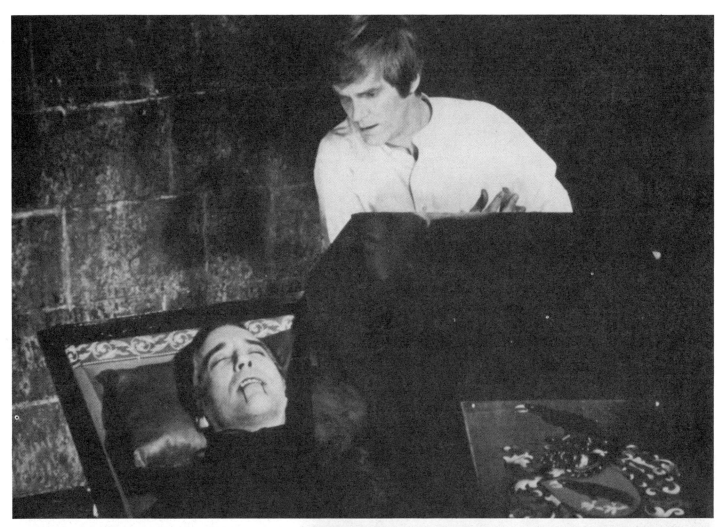

The vampire's resting place is very sacred to the nocturnal beast. No trespassers are welcomed. Opposite Top: Count Dracula (John Carradine) warns Onslow Stevens not to tamper with his coffin in HOUSE OF DRACULA (1945); Opposite Bottom: Christopher Lee and his mistress rest during daylight hours in TASTE THE BLOOD OF DRACULA (1969); Top: Christopher Matthews unfortunately discovers Dracula's resting place in SCARS OF DRACULA (1970); Right: Annette Vadin is about to locate her lesbian-vampire-lover in BLOOD AND ROSES (1960).

Not all vampires are handsome, polished gentlemen; some vampires are truly hideous! Top: David Peel's vampire Baron Meinster was once pretty until his face was splashed with holy water in BRIDES OF DRACULA (1960); Left: A grotesque vampire from FRIGHT NIGHT II (1988); Opposite Top Left: The monstrous human vampire from VOODOO HEARTBEAT (1972); Opposite Top Right: Vampire Chris Sarandon shows his true face in FRIGHT NIGHT (1985); Opposite Bottom: The screen's most hideous and foul vampire from NOSFERATU (1979).

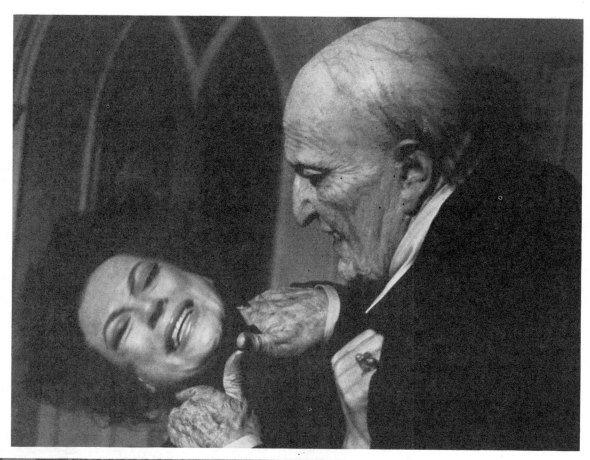

Never find yourself caught at the mercy of a vampire, as illustrated in the following stills. Top: from HOUSE OF DARK SHADOWS (1970); Left: from SON OF DRACULA (1943); Below: from HOUSE OF DARK SHADOWS (1970); Opposite Top: from DRACULA – PRINCE OF DARKNESS (1965); Opposite Bottom: from COUNT YORGA – VAMPIRE (1970).

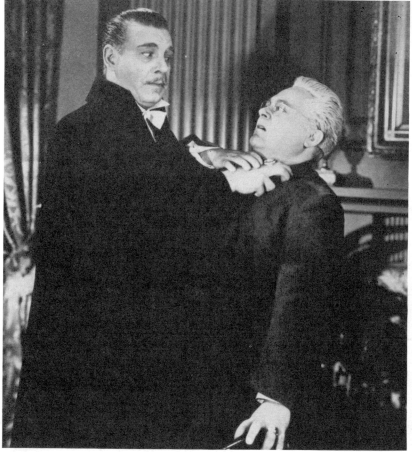

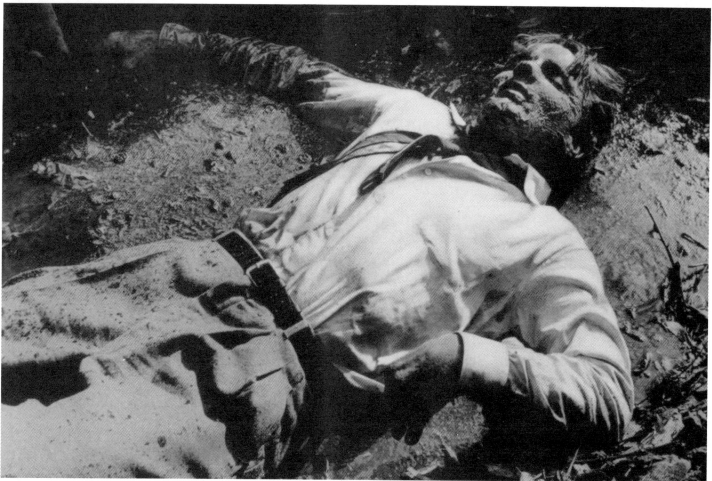

Killing a vampire is not an easy task, and the death of one of these nocturnal creatures is not a pretty sight. Opposite Top: Barbara Shelley rests in peace after a wooden stake is driven through her heart in DRACULA – PRINCE OF DARKNESS (1965); Opposite Bottom: Vampire John Beal begins to decompose during the climax of THE VAMPIRE (1957); Top: Vampire Killer Peter Cushing decapitates the head of Mircalla in Hammer's THE VAMPIRE LOVERS (1970); Right: Christopher Lee begins to decompose into a bloody mess during the climax of DRACULA A.D. – 1972 (1971).

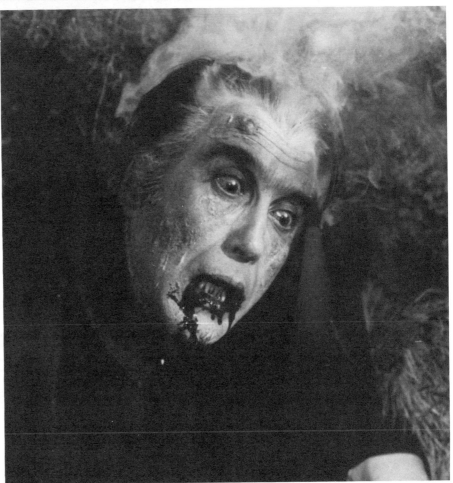

Today's vampire is far removed from the traditional creatures of the night. Top: The cab-driving vampire of GRAVEYARD SHIFT (1987) is about to claim another victim; Left: A very bizarre-looking creature of the night from FRIGHT NIGHT II (1988); Opposite Top: The modern vampire clan from NEAR DARK (1987); Opposite Bottom: The modern vampires from THE LOST BOYS (1987) display how savage today's species really are.

86

Hollywood has created numerous funny and offbeat vampire characters. Opposite Top Left: George Hamilton plays an outgoing traditional Dracula in a modern New York in LOVE AT FIRST BITE (1979); Opposite Top Right: Even Bela Lugosi spoofed his own Dracula characterizations from time to time. Here the actor portrays an eccentric scientist who thinks he is actually a vampire in OLD MOTHER RILEY MEETS THE VAMPIRE (1952); Opposite Bottom: Comedians Abbott and Costello are trapped by both Dracula (Bela Lugosi) and the Frankenstein Monster (Glenn Strange) in ABBOTT AND COSTELLO MEET FRANKENSTEIN (1948); Top: Grace Jones as the very offbeat but lethal vampiress Katrina in VAMP (1986); Right: The late David Niven as Old Dracula in VAMPIRA (1973).

Hollywood usually depicts the vampire as a savage, bloodthirsty beast. Top: One of the savage, blood-craved vampires from THE LOST BOYS (1987); Left: Count Dracula (Christopher Lee) gets physical with his mistress in HORROR OF DRACULA (1958); Opposite Top: A sultry female vampire displays her savage side in SCARS OF DRACULA (1970); Opposite Bottom: The first victim of Barnabas Collins rises from her grave to become a savage vampire in HOUSE OF DARK SHADOWS (1970).

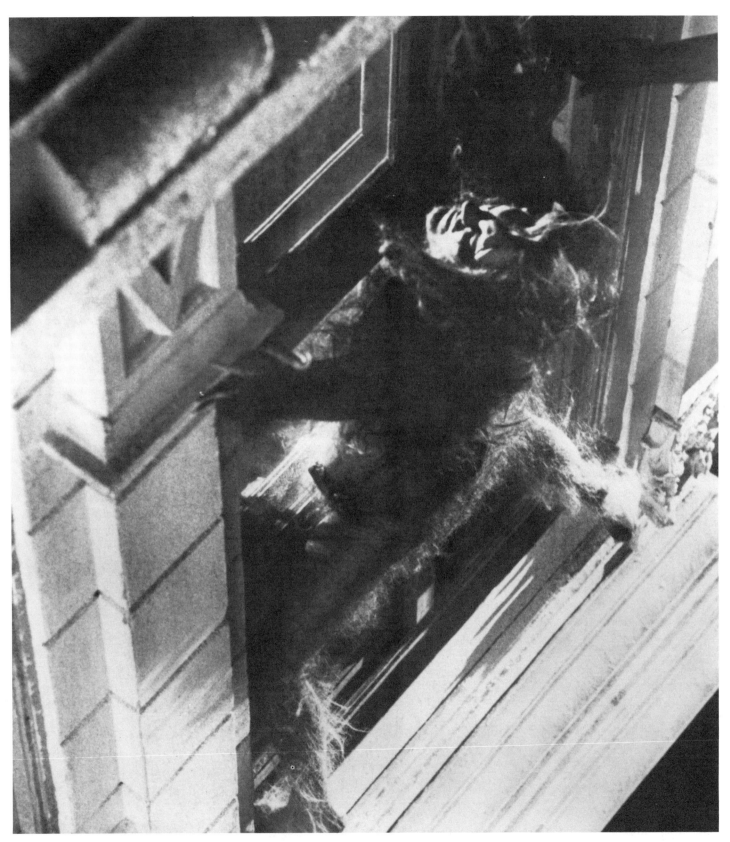

Vampires on the loose! Opposite Top: A six foot vampire bat goes on a rampage in FRIGHT NIGHT (1985); Opposite Bottom: The film's hero desperately fends off the advance of three vampire brides in THE MONSTER SQUAD (1987); Top: The hideous vampire transformed-werewolf climbs up the side of a building in FRIGHT NIGHT II (1988).

How many different ways can a vampire be destroyed? Top: Count Orlock dies at the mercy of the sun's rays in NOSFERATU (1922); Left: A sultry vampiress finds her death when Peter Cushing decapitates her in TWINS OF EVIL (1972); Opposite Top: Count Dracula (Chris Lee) discovers how much damage a little running water can do during the climax of DRACULA PRINCE OF DARKNESS (1965); Opposite Bottom Left: Chris Lee is impaled by a silver spike in DRACULA A.D. 1972 (1971); Opposite Bottom Right: Gloria Holden is destroyed by a wooden arrow in DRACULA'S DAUGHTER (1936).

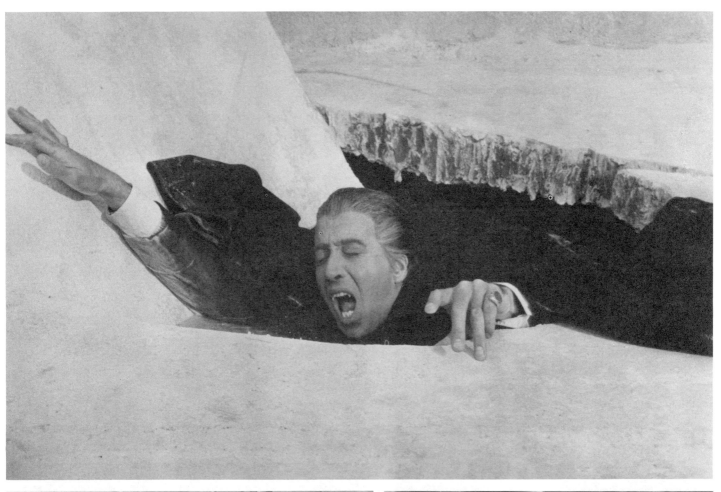

The vampire always gets his girl!
Opposite Top Left: Dracula
(Christopher Lee) seduces Veronica
Carlson in DRACULA HAS RISEN FROM
THE GRAVE (1968); Opposite Top Right:
Bela Lugosi makes his move on his
intended female victim in MARK OF THE
VAMPIRE (1935); Opposite Bottom
Left: Humphrey Bogart as a vampiric
Dr. X in THE RETURN OF DR. X (1939);
Opposite Bottom Right: Frank Langella
seduces his victim into vampirism in
DRACULA (1979); Top: Christopher
Lee shows us how to get his girl by
physical means in HORROR OF DRACULA
(1958); Right: David Peel carries on
the age-old tradition of vampire
meets girl; vampire bites girl in
BRIDES OF DRACULA (1960).

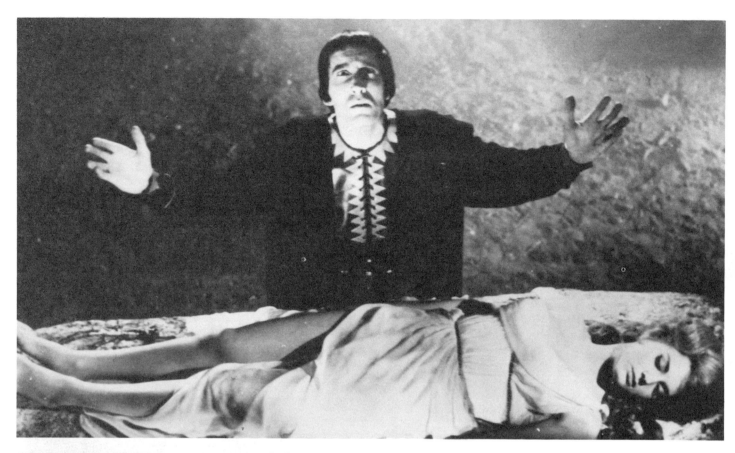

You must always be on guard when a vampire offers his hand. This gesture only spells doom for the victim. Top: Christopher Lee as Lico the vampire stretches his arms out in HERCULES IN THE HAUNTED WORLD (1966); Left: Kiefer Sutherland – vampire, offers his hand of death in THE LOST BOYS (1987); Below: Gloria Holden in the title role of DRACULA'S DAUGHTER (1936); Opposite: Francis Lederer as Count Dracula offers his hands as a gesture of good will – but we know better! From THE RETURN OF DRACULA (1958).

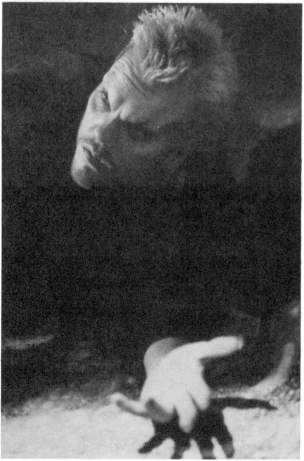

CD(17-2)-12

The victim of a vampire usually encounters death and sometimes inevitable transformation into a bloodsucker. Top: Dracula (Christopher Lee) inflicts pain upon his manservant in SCARS OF DRACULA (1970); Left: Pseudo-vampire Bela Lugosi frightens his victims in MARK OF THE VAMPIRE (1935); Opposite Top: John Van Eyssen painfully discovers that he is the victim of a vampire in HORROR OF DRACULA (1958); Opposite Bottom: Vampire and gunslinger Drake Roby carries off the film's heroine in THE UNEARTHLY (1959).

Some vampires can be very fierce and frightening to behold. Top: Barlow, the savage, hideous vampire from SALEM'S LOT (1979); Left: Christopher Lee's Count Dracula displays his savage personalities in COUNT DRACULA (1970); Below: Dracula ruthlessly feeds on Isabelle Adjani in NOSFERATU (1979); Opposite: Russell Clark bares her lethal fangs in FRIGHT NIGHT II (1988).

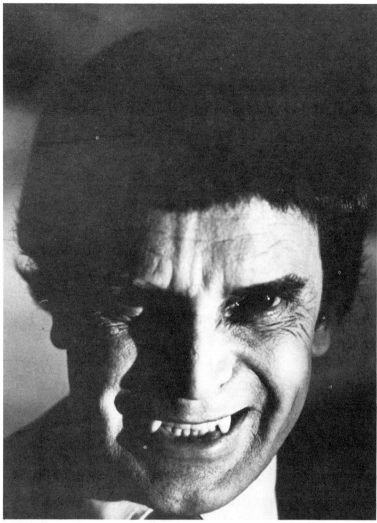

Master vampires come in all guises. *Top Left: Baron Meinster from BRIDES OF DRACULA (1960); Top Right: Janos Skorzeny- vampire from NIGHT STALKER (1972); Bottom Left: Richard Lynch from VAMPIRE (1979); Above: From Sylvia Kristel as DRACULA'S WIDOW (1988); Opposite: Barnabas Collins - master vampire from HOUSE OF DARK SHADOWS (1970).*

The lavish vampire film is as extinct as the dinosair. The larger-than life sets, elaborate costumes and eerie atmosphere are the trademarks of the lavish vampire film. Top: The most elaborate of all vampire classics is DRACULA (1931), with its magnificent sets and strong atmospheric photography; Left: Elaborate sets and costumes were used to create the dream-like effect for MARK OF THE VAMPIRE (1935); Opposite: LONDON AFTER MIDNIGHT (1927) was one of the first of the expensive and lavish vampire films from Hollywood.

Good against evil is the common denominator in any good vampire film! Opposite: Bela Lugosi is confronted by the powers of goodness when his werewolf servant turns to the righteous side in RETURN OF THE VAMPIRE (1943); Top: Investigative reporter Carl Kolchak confronts the evil vampire Janos Skorzeny in NIGHT STALKER (1972); Right: Are the powers of goodness a match for the sultry and seductive Mircalla in LUST FOR A VAMPIRE (1971)?

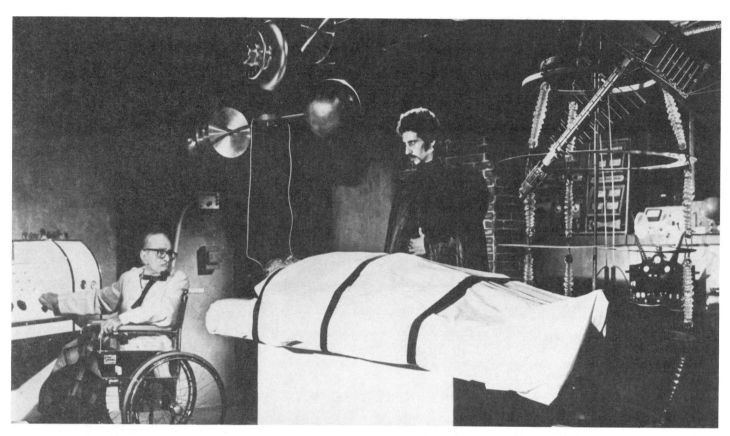

"DRACULA
VERSUS
FRANKENSTEIN"
Starring
MICHAEL RENNIE · KARIN DOR
CRAIG HILL
Eastmancolour

Whenever Count Dracula meets the Frankenstein Monster, a fierce battle always ensues, Opposite Top: Count Dracula (Zandor Vorkov) and mad scientist J. Carrol Naish have great plans of resurrecting the Frankenstein Monster in DRACULA VS. FRANKENSTEIN (1972); Opposite Bottom: Dracula (skeleton with wooden stake in heart) is about to meet the Wolfman and the Frankenstein Monster in THE MAN WHO CAME FROM UMMO (1970); Top: Dracula and the Frankenstein Monster engaged in a fierce battle to the end in DRACULA VS. FRANKENSTEIN (1972); Right: Dracula (Bela Lugosi) has plans of using the Frankenstein Monster (Glenn Strange) to conquer the world in ABBOTT AND COSTELLO MEET FRANKENSTEIN (1948).

Attack of more vampires! Opposite
Top: Dracula (Jack Palance)
agressively claims another victim in
DRACULA (1973); Opposite Bottom:
Countess Elizabeth Bathory (Ingrid
Pitt) goes berserk with dagger in
hand in Hammer's COUNTESS
DRACULA (1971); Top: Bela Lugosi
as Dracula attacks heroine Helen
Chandler in Universal's DRACULA
(1931); Right: Vampire at large in
VAMPIRA (1973).

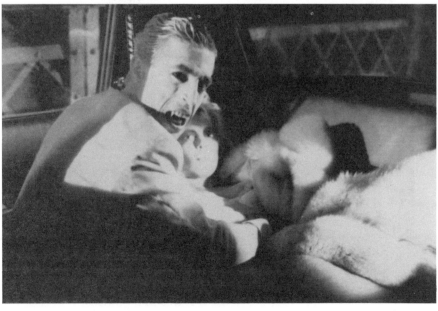

One last Bite! Top: Good old Barnabas Collins quenches human blood to restore his more youthful appearance in HOUSE OF DARK SHADOWS (1970); Left: for a three hundred and fifty year old vampire who drives a cab in New York City, terror is his favorite passenger. from GRAVEYARD SHIFT (1987); Opposite Top: Christopher Lee has plans of making Barbara Shelley his mistress in DRACULA- PRINCE OF DARKNESS (1965); Opposite Bottom: finally, Dracula's hound chomps down on a fresh victim in DRACULA'S DOG (1975).

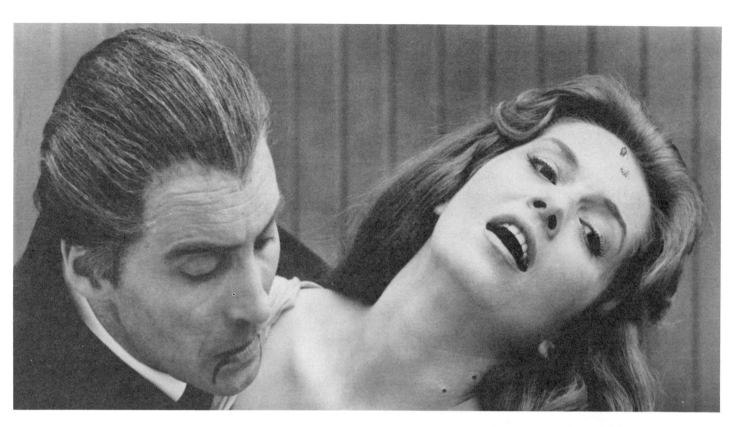

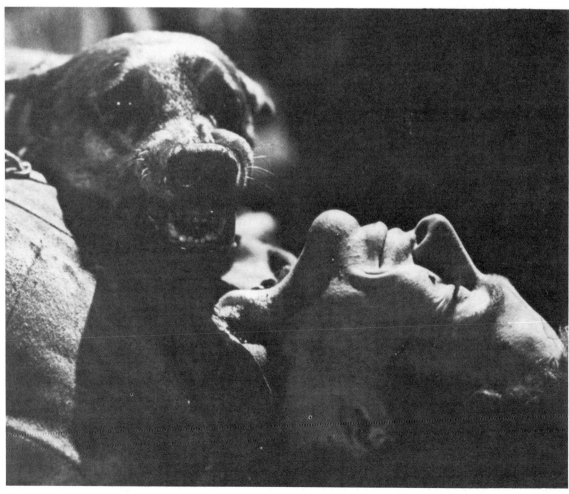

AFTERWARDS

I have experienced great pleasures while writing this book. For me, the vampire film is my favorite genre of horror films. I literally love a good vampire movie; thus the inspiration for writing this guide. I must mention once again that I have tried to cover every vampire film known to exist, however, I am sure I have missed a few films along the way. I have also tried to cover the most recent vampire films, but because of deadlines, I was unable to cover many of the new vampire films released just before and shortly after the November 1992 publication date of this book. Because of this unfortunate case of bad timing, I have added this little section to record the direction the genre is scheduled to take within the coming months.

Restrictions and deadlines only allowed me to review BUFFY THE VAMPIRE SLAYER (1992) as the last entry to this book. As early as August 1992, news was circulating about Francis Ford Coppola's new version of the Bram Stoker novel entitled BRAM STOKER'S DRACULA. In various interviews, Coppola assured horror film fans that the new film would most certainly be a horror film rather than just another adaptation of a Gothic classic. It is also common knowledge that actor Anthony Hopkins was cast as Abraham Van Helsing, the famous vampire-killer, while Gary Oldman was cast as Count Dracula, a true characterization of the legendary warrior and infamous vampire. The cast also included Winona Ryder as Mina and young Keanu Reeves as Jonathan Harker, who makes that timeless voyage to Transylvania. From what I have been able to gather as of this writing from a combination of previews, interviews, and magazines articles, BRAM STOKER'S DRACULA promises to be Fall of 1992's major blockbuster and perhaps the most refreshing version of the timeless Bram Stoker story since Hammer's masterpiece HORROR OF DRACULA, release in 1958. I somehow feel that this film will surpass our expectations and I hope that I will be able to write good comments about this film when I update this book in five years or so.

1992 promises to be a grand year on the bloodsucker genre. Not since 1970 has the vampire film received so much attention. There is no doubt that revival of vampire films is certainly upon us. To date and as of this writing, there are two dozen vampire films currently scheduled for release or undergoing filming for a 1993 release. Among the films currently in release or scheduled for release is MY GRANDPA IS A VAMPIRE (1992), a $1.4 million New Zealand-made film starring Al (Grandpa-Munster) Lewis as 300 year-old vampire Vernon T. Cooger. I have not yet had a chance to review this film but from the sound of it, I would reckon that Lewis' vampire will no doubt be reminiscent of his previous vampire characterization of Grandpa Munster from the television sit-com THE MUNSTERS.

TALE OF A VAMPIRE appears to be another promising vampire tale scheduled for release in the near horizon. The film is scheduled to star modern horror star Julian (WARLOCK and ARACHNOPHOBIA) Sands as a lonely vampire named Alex and Suzanna Hamilton is cast as the heroine who falls under the vampire's spell. Apparently, the film is supposed to be quite the opposite of and totally removed from the usual vampire trappings.

Then there is INNOCENT BLOOD, another enthusiastic-sounding vampire film from John Landis. The film is Landis' first genre film since his cult classic AN AMERICAN WEREWOLF IN LONDON which was released way back in 1981 and is supposedly a film about vampire gangsters. INNOCENT BLOOD is planned to mix horror with occasional laughs.

TO SLEEP WITH A VAMPIRE is also scheduled for a late 1992- early 1993 release. The film, directed by Adam Friedman, is a Roger Corman production that stars Scott Valentine as the lead vampire. The film promises to be bloody, but Corman's other upcoming vampire film, DRACULA RISING, promises to be a superior effort. In this film Christopher Atkins is scheduled to star as Dracula and the film is supposedly Corman's flip-side of his previous FRANKENSTEIN UNBOUND, combining time travel with the Dracula legend. I really look forward to this film.

Republic Pictures is back on the scene announcing 99 DAYS, a film about a psychic who is bitten by a vampire and has exactly 99 days to stop his transformation into a bloodsucker. Other vampire films announced are: IN THE MIDNIGHT HOUR about a schizophrenic vampire who moonlights as a rock and roll pop star; SUBSPECIES II from Full Moon Entertainment promises to feature Andres Hove as the hideous skeleton-like vampire named Radu under the same direction of Ted Nicolaou; VALERIE is an independent film about a lesbian vampire; and THE RELUCTANT VAMPIRE is scheduled to star Adam Ant in the title role.

The recent boom in vampire movies is an indication that the genre is alive and kicking better than ever. The fact that Columbia Pictures has invested over $40 million into the production of BRAM STOKER'S DRACULA indicates that executives are banking on a multi-million dollar box-office smash hit, which I believe will inspire other motion picture companies to invest more money into many new and exciting vampire films. Don't be surprised if the new Francis Coppola film sparks new life into the genre and dozens of new vampire films begin appearing from every direction. If this happens, I may be updating this book sooner than five years!

THERE'S MORE TO THE LEGEND
THAN MEETS... THE THROAT!

Dracula's Dog

FILM INDEX

The following is an alphabetical listing of all the vampire movies that can be found in this book.

ACKNOWLEDGMENTS

Many people contributed in the preparation of this new book on vampire movies. First, I must thank the closest people around me, my family, who put up with a lot of crap from me while I was putting this book together. Thank you Mom and Dad for your patience. Thank you Andrew Davies for your understanding and patience. Thanks to my friends who could not wait to see the finished product. Secondly, I would like to thank Jerry Ohlinger's Movie Material Store and The Book and Poster Company for their assistance in locating some of the photos contained in this book. Finally, I would like to thank artist Scott Jones for designing the cover of this book. Without each of you, this book would not be possible.

ABOUT THE AUTHOR

Robert Marrero, author of DRACULA - THE VAMPIRE LEGEND ON FILM, is, in his words, a very serious film enthusiast and researcher of fantastic movies. Marrero has studied the history of fantastic cinema from his early adulthood days and has published several books on horror films, including VAMPIRES- HAMMER STYLE, HORRORS OF HAMMER and NIGHTMARE THEATER, the latter considered an illustrated guide to the horror film. Currently Marrero owns and manages The Douglas House, a charming, Victorian-style bed and breakfast on the island of Key West, Florida, where he is hard at work on his next project. To make reservations at The Douglas House in Key West you can call 1-800-833-0372.